RECORD STORE DAYS

RECORD STORE DAYS

FROM VINYL TO DIGITAL AND BACK AGAIN

Gary Calamar and Phil Gallo

SCOTT CALAMAR, EDITOR

STERLING
New York

STERLING
New York

An Imprint of Sterling Publishing
387 Park Avenue South
New York, NY 10016

ISBN 978-1-4027-7232-0 (hardcover)
ISBN 978-1-4027-9455-1 (paperback)

Distributed in Canada by Sterling Publishing
c/o Canadian Manda Group, 165 Dufferin Street
Toronto, Ontario, Canada M6K 3H6
Distributed in the United Kingdom by GMC Distribution Services
Castle Place, 166 High Street, Lewes, East Sussex, England BN7 1XU
Distributed in Australia by Capricorn Link (Australia) Pty. Ltd.
P.O. Box 704, Windsor, NSW 2756, Australia

Packaged by LightSpeed Publishing, Inc.
Interior design by X-Height Studio

Photo credits on page 226 constitute an extension of this copyright page.

For information about custom editions, special sales, and premium and corporate
purchases, please contact Sterling Special Sales at 800-805-5489 or
specialsales@sterlingpublishing.com.

Manufactured in China

10 9 8 7 6 5 4 3 2 1

www.sterlingpublishing.com

In memory of
Ronny Calamar

FOREWORD

WHEN I WAS 13, I started listening to underground radio, grew my hair long, and hung around a record store. We had just moved to Georgia and I didn't know anybody there, but I decided it was a cool place.

One day I approached the guys who worked there—they were all in their 20s, with shoulder-length hair and walrus mustaches—and said, "Say, listen. I will clean up and do whatever you want me to do if you will give me a discount—sell me records at your price." That way I would get discounts on records that I really liked and then say that I worked there. It was maybe three hours of work a week, but

This Columbia Records retailer from the early 20th century sold pianos and other musical items.

I got to hang out there 10 hours a week and tell my friends that I worked in a record store.

Having the job didn't make me hip, but it gave me something to do, something to talk about, people to meet. It was also a way to learn about all this stuff.

In those days, the stores were smaller and a complete reflection of the people who ran them. The owners could be really fun or really cranky and weird. The stores could be obscure and off-putting, or totally open; each had its own aesthetic. Having someone curate a store made it easy to acquire records that you might never have heard about otherwise.

I was working at Wuxtry Records in Athens, Georgia, which was mostly a used store. Michael Stipe was in the store a lot. I think he was buying a Suicide record that got me to talking to him. He was looking to form a band; I was looking to form a band. It worked out.

As I went around the country with R.E.M., there were stores the size of my bedroom full of good stuff that was all specially ordered. People tend to forget there was a period in which records by a popular band like The Yardbirds were hardly available. Before the Internet, it was all about prowling record stores, looking at fanzines, and, on occasion, ordering singles from England that might show up in three months or possibly never at all.

I'm fortunate to live in Seattle where there are three great stores I frequent.

Easy Street is the huge one and I walk there, usually once a week. Sonic Boom is a great place for indies. Off the Wall is more avant-garde—free jazz, great electronic stuff—it's more of a curated place. I could go and get pretty much anything at the first two, and go to Off the Wall for super-obscure ethnic records, Japanese free jazz pressings.

I'll probably walk to the store today.

Peter Buck
July 2009

ACKNOWLEDGMENTS

T HIS BOOK WOULD not be possible without the help of people who facilitated interviews and assisted in unearthing the history: James Bailey, Cary Baker, Bill Bentley, Bertis Downs, Mike Grimes, Michael Kurtz, Anna Loynes, Keith McCarthy, Bob Merlis, Dawn Novak, Kevin O'Neil, Hannah Pantle, Amanda Pitts, Ben Weber, and Yvette Ziraldo.

Thank you to everyone who provided their time, anecdotes, photographs, and opinions: Ryan Adams, CC Adcock, Dave Alvin, Josh Anderson, Eli Attie, Jimmy B, Ilene Barg, Bob Bell, Patrick Belton, Danny Benair, Steve Bergman, Tom Biery, Colin Blunstone, John Brassil, John Brenes, Debbie Brewer, Harold Bronson, Del Bryant, Peter Buck, David Budge, Neal Casal, Peter Case, Matthew Caws, Lee Cohen, James Combs, Brian Corona, Keith Covart, Stephanie Covart, Zac Cowie, Cameron Crowe, Terry Currier, John Darnielle, Doyle Davis, Jeff Davis, Henry Deas, John Debold, Marcia Calamar Diamond, Henry Diltz, John Doe, Mike Dreese, Nadine DuBois, Paul Epstein, Sam Epstein, Richard Foos, Michele Fleischli, Rand Foster, Bruce Lee Gallanter, John George, Randy Gerston, Cary Ginell, Daniel Glass, John Goddard, Tom Gracyk, Jim Greenwood, Gerald Hamill, Vicky Hamilton, David Henderson, John Heneghan, Gary Helsinger, Doug Herzog, David Hirschland, Robyn Hitchcock, Susanna Hoffs, Tricia Holloway, Peter Holsapple, Wayne Holznagel, John Huffman, Lyle Hysen, Eric Isaacson, Peter and Jennifer Jesperson, Kevin Johnson, Ira Kaplan, Lenny Kaye, Dan Kennedy, Matt Kivel, Howie Klein, Bob Koester, Mark Kozelek, Jason Kramer, John Kunz, Kimber Lanning, Edmund Lestrange, Eric Levin, Peter Liebert, Jen Malone, Cary Mansfield, Larry

Marion, Manny Maris, Michael McCollum, Orion Meyer, Hale Milgrim, Eve Monsees, Howie Muira, Julie Muncy, Ron Murray, Laura O'Neill, Philip L. Newman, Miwa Okumura, Chuck Prophet, Lisa Ray, Henry Rollins, Gene Rumsey, Duncan Scheidt, Neil Schield, Andy Schwartz, Nancy Sefton, Mike Shalett, Ron Shapiro, Michael Shelley, Tim Soter, Ed Stasium, Gary Stewart, Kit "Stymee" Stovepipe, Russ Solomon, Matthew Sweet, John Timmons, Chris Vanderloo, Ben Vaughan, Robert Vickers, Michelle Wallace, Jerry Weber, Marc Weinstein, Howard Weulfing, Lucinda Williams, Josh Wittman, Rick Wojcik, Adam Wolf, Steve Wynn, and Marc and Debra Zakarin.

Phil Gallo would like to thank Gary Calamar for establishing an inviting work relationship and editor Scott Calamar for playing the role of watchdog, wordsmith, therapist, and cheerleader. Thanks also to Steve Mirkin for recommending me for the job. And to my daughters Monica and Laura, thanks for your support and understanding. At the top of the list is my wife, Betsy, whose support, encouragement, and love enrich my life daily. Without her, not only would the world be a dark and cold place, I would not be following my dreams. And special thanks to my parents, who let me spend all of my allowance on records and an inordinate amount of time in record stores.

Gary Calamar would like to thank Alyson Vidoli for holding down the fort at GO Music while I played around with this book. Our extremely talented and patient editor Scott "Cousin Scotty" Calamar. Love and thanks to my mother, Penny Calamar, for taking me to see *A Hard Day's Night* in 1964 and my brother Ronny for explaining it to me. And the two loves of my life: my beautiful wife, Ali, who rocks me in a very similar fashion to that of a hurricane, and my daughter Zoe, who is the coolest person I know. Special thanks to Phil Gallo who makes great writing and impossible deadlines look easy.

Scott Calamar of LightSpeed Publishing would like to give additional heartfelt thanks to designer Cecile Kaufman for bringing these pages to life, as she always does, under the pressures of impossible deadlines; and to DQ Johnson for her speed, attention to detail, and helpfulness. Kudos go out to David Henderson, John Huffman, and Wayne Holznagel, as well as other collectors, for their extra effort with photographs. I would also like to thank my dad, Art, whose love of Big Bands has been an ongoing musical inspiration.

The authors and packager would like to thank Myrsini Stephanides for signing this book; and Michael Fragnito and Jason Prince of Sterling Publishing for allowing us to see it through.

INTRODUCTION

FOR THOSE WHO WORK IN record stores, or those who can't wait to steal a little time from their day to hang out in record shops, Tuesday is the best day of the week.

There may be hype about the weekend for many of us, but Tuesday is the traditional New Release day at the record store. All record stores. Coast to coast. Sea to shining sea. Then and now. Tuesday is when the latest gift from your favorite artist comes rolling through the record store delivery door. A hand truck full of hits! A cardboard carton filled with copies of a new classic!

Record Store Days has been germinated from two distinct points of view, essentially both sides of the counter. Each of us has his own set of experiences that brought us together to collaborate on this project. We both love record stores and we're both passionate about the roles they've played in our lives.

Gary spent the late '70s and all of the 1980s at legendary Southern California shops such as Rhino Records, Moby Disc, and Licorice Pizza. Phil is strictly an avid shopper who has come perilously close to falling into the category of collector.

Gary's epiphany dates back to 1964. By age 12, his brother Ronny, who was three years his senior, had a firm handle on the hippest, most happening sounds exploding from the '60s pop music scene. Sitting around the breakfast table, Ronny spoke endlessly about the Spinning Disc, a record store he would visit in the Bronx. He would regularly return home from the Spinning Disc with a single (or LP!) by an exciting new artist such as the Beatles, the Rolling Stones, Marianne Faithfull, the Beach Boys, or the Zombies. He'd slap it on the family stereo and bang!

Ronny was allowed to travel to the Bronx, via bus and subway, from the family's Yonkers apartment. Unfortunately, Gary was deemed too young to adventure in such a fashion. One Saturday morning, Ronny snuck Gary down the fire escape, over to the subway station, and into a brave new world! It was Gary's first subway ride and his first visit to the Spinning Disc! He was thrilled and a little scared...

Walking through the door of the Spinning Disc, Gary could not believe his eyes or ears. The store's walls were plastered with countless colorful album and single sleeves. Promo posters showed longhaired boys in outrageous outfits gripping electric guitars! The store's record player blasted "Glad All Over" by the Dave Clark Five. Some cool-looking teenager with Beatle-bangs ignored Gary from behind the counter and his whole world fell away. After flipping through the singles racks, and agonizing between so many choices, Gary made his very first record purchase: "All Day and All of the Night" b/w (backed with) "I Gotta Move" by The Kinks on Reprise records.

As he got older, Gary's obsession continued—he could not pass a record store without paying a visit to his vinyl friends in the bins. Later, upon moving to Los Angeles, he could not believe his luck when he landed a job at Licorice Pizza Records And Tapes, where he was exposed to many of his favorite artists, and relished in talking music with the customers and fellow employees.

Phil's obsession started at the age of 10 when he bought Cream's *Disraeli Gears* for $1.97 at a shop on a beach in Oregon, and most recently included the acquisition of picture-sleeve 45s by Petula Clark in Nice, France. He cannot forget the store in London that sold only reggae 45s and required a train, a bus, and a half-mile walk to get there. There was a summer he spent moving from one friend's spare bed to another in Santa Barbara, but his homelessness did not stop him from buying records by Tom Waits, Jonathan Richman, NRBQ, and Ralph Towner at Morninglory Music.

Record stores in the San Fernando Valley, New York, and New Jersey became schools that educated Phil about artists and genres. As much as they presented goods for sale, they offered mysteries and puzzles that could only be solved by expanding the search for records in used record shops, flea markets, swap meets, record fairs, used bins, and garage sales. That was about the bargain, the thrill of the hunt, the landing of a holy grail in a garage, a dusty field, or the back of a used furniture store.

Without record stores, there would be far less joy in our lives. We've tasted their transcendent buzz, and are now joyously, irredeemably addicted. We go to the record store for our fix. To people like us, downloading feels like musical methadone.

It's nice to reflect on the good times we've all

had in these shops, but let's not focus entirely backwards. Record Store Days are here and now, occupied by smaller, boutique shops that are owned, staffed, and patronized by real music lovers looking for real music. Ironically, the technology that helped dismantle the mass record industry has helped us to circle back to an earlier, simpler, and more intimate time—a time when all record shops were independent little ventures run by music fans for music fans. Great record stores in nearly every city are still going strong and doing a great job keeping the music available and the connections between music lovers alive.

Record stores came of age in the late 1960s, a time when America was in a state of revolution. The underground record stores that sprang up in New York, San Francisco, and Los Angeles became models for stores in cities and towns across the country. By the early '70s, no matter where you were, the record store was the coolest place on the block. In some instances, it was because of the bootlegs and, in other cases, it may have been the bongs, but ultimately it was the passion for the music that kept people coming in.

Music fans became entrepreneurs, following the model created by jazz fans of the 1940s and '50s when they opted to enter retail. Despite format changes, staggering inflation, and competition from various angles, many great record stores have remained standing. The first decade of the 21st century has brought considerable change

in the way music has been consumed, but it continues to attract adventurers willing to stick their necks out to bring music in a physical form to fans. The record store is by no means extinct. If anything, maybe it is even more treasured.

In the '70s, the great record shopping city of America might have been Berkeley, California, or maybe Boston. There are votes for Chicago and Hollywood, Philadelphia and Pittsburgh, Minneapolis and the suburbs of D.C. There's a sense of ownership—having a great record store, to the people involved in this industry in the 20th century, was as much a point of civic pride as a great baseball team, orchestra, and museum. At its core, it is a business with a product to sell, but there is not another consumer good with the emotional attraction of the LP.

Stories included here are unique in their specifics but universal in their generality. A recounted story from Austin, Texas, or the suburbs of Chicago is likely to be just as true as one from Seattle or Miami. Record-buying conjures so many shared memories, it feels as if it had once been a ritual for all the practitioners: searching cutout bins and used shops for bargains; dropping in on a hip store daily to inquire about new releases; finding the import specialist; taking the advice of the clerk and buying that record he or she insists you just must have.

It's not a glamorous business, but it has its air of mystique, especially for anyone who, as a young person, ventured into the great hole-in-the-wall stores of the 1960s and '70s. They didn't use the word back then, but any retailer that opted to carry records beyond the latest hits was obviously curating their store, a trend of the 21st century that has made record shopping once again fun.

Our senses work overtime when we enter a record store—we take in the posters, mobiles, and artwork on the CD and LP covers, not to mention the sounds booming over the sound system. One woman we spoke to swears that Tom Petty's *Damn The Torpedoes* is the best smelling album. Something about the red ink. Where would we be without the record store? What if Brian Epstein had chosen to run a flower shop instead of the NEMS store in Liverpool? What if Peter Buck never struck up a conversation with Michael Stipe at Wuxtry in Athens? Would the musical world be the same as we now know it?

Conducting interviews for this book was like joining a club. Most of the people in the record store business share an enthusiasm for vinyl, a passion for collecting, and a belief in the creative spirit. They look for a connection to the artistry and physical recordings to fill a part of that need. The goods are tactile. They prompt visceral responses and in most cases, no other commercial object has that power to stimulate the mind or the soul.

Phil's wife is fond of saying that the happiest he looks in any photograph is in one taken at the Jazz Record Mart in Chicago. There's something about being in your element, surrounded by the familiar and the unknown, which great record stores provide. There may certainly be places we enjoy more, but somehow a record store just represents a comfort zone unlike any other.

To paraphrase Ray Davies from the Kinks, who penned the first song Gary purchased:

"God Save Record Shops, the phonolog, and variety."

Now let's go shopping.

Support Your Local Record Store
For more information visit: recordstoreday.com, thealliancerocks.com, cimsmusic.com, musicmonitornetwork.com

RECORD STORE DAYS

THE HOUSE
IS A-ROCKIN'

A CAPACITY CROWD of about 800 fans watched Elvis Costello perform at Amoeba Music in Hollywood on June 22, 2009. The crowd was packed in, yet orderly, standing in dozens of aisles created by permanent bins holding compacts discs and vinyl albums.

Costello was appearing the night before his album *Secret, Profane & Sugarcane* would be released. It was his 26th studio album in 33 years, a sign of a prolific artist, and it paid off—the album debuted at No. 13, Costello's highest chart position since 1980.

Certainly a coup to book a person of Costello's stature for a free concert, the performance was his second that day.

The continuing romance of music fans and the great record stores has endured for a century

In Hollywood in June 2009, Elvis Costello promoted *Secret, Profane & Sugarcane* the night before its release with an in-store performance and an autograph session.

The gimmick to promote this album, his first for the Hear/Concord label, was for Costello to play a lunchtime set at the San Francisco Amoeba Music before jetting to L.A. to perform for an hour in the evening.

As is customary, Costello would hang around to sign the new album, released on CD and LP, as well as the promotional poster. Throughout the night, his appearance at the 5,700-seat Greek Theater in August was promoted via stage announcements.

The event brought unique energy to Amoeba, a block-long CD, LP, and DVD warehouse of a store that fronts Sunset Boulevard and is bordered by Cahuenga and Ivar. Its neighbor to the east is the famed Cinerama Dome movie theater; to the west on Sunset are storefronts that cater to fans of Hollywood lore and memorabilia, mixed with the occasional business that provides services to the recording industry.

Opened in November 2001, the 43,000-square-foot shop has become the new model for the music superstore. Independently owned, rich in back catalog, almost equally stocked in used and new products, and filled with employees who obsess about bands, records, and concerts, it is the store that other stores aspire to become in the 21st century.

While Costello was performing, the 20th century model of a music superstore was being given a wake just two blocks away at a bar that was once a major music industry hangout. The Virgin Megastore, created by Richard Branson, was a vision that had worked well at times, but once the real estate company that held the stores' leases took over, they decided that music retail was the wrong business for them.

The wake, attended by the company's final two CEOs and various alumni, was low-key. Obviously, the loss of jobs created heavy hearts, but there was also the searing reality that jobs at record stores, an employment choice more often made from a point of passion rather than logic, would not be available elsewhere.

The music business hit a high back in 2000 and sales slipped 45 percent over the next eight years;

> "I love all the things about the *B* section in the record store, which is why it was important that we were named the Bangles. It was really a big deal when we got a card with our name and we weren't just in the random *B*s."
>
> —SUSANNA HOFFS

the owners of the Virgin buildings knew that other businesses were better suited to pay higher rents.

The last Megastores, located in Union Square in New York, and inside the complex that holds the home of the Academy Awards—the Kodak Theater, in Hollywood—were shuttered on June 14, 2009. *The New York Times* eulogized the shuttering of the New York home, noting that it left the city devoid of a major music retail chain.

FINAL WEEKS!
HOLLYWOOD & HIGHLAND LOCATION ONLY!

Virgin MEGASTORE

STORE CLOSING!

NEW PRICE CUTS!

40-60% OFF
ORIG. PRICES

EVERYTHING!
TIME IS RUNNING OUT!

40% OFF ORIG. PRICES
ALL
CAMERAS, ELECTRONICS, PHONES, HEADPHONES, MP3 ACCESSORIES, TOYS, ACTION FIGURES, T-SHIRTS, TOPS, HATS, TOTES, BELTS, MESSENGER BAGS

40% OFF ORIG. PRICES
ALL
CD'S, DVD'S, BLU-RAY, VINYLS, BOOKS

60% OFF ORIG. PRICES
ALL
JEWELRY, BODY JEWELRY, WALLETS, HINT BOOKS, KEY CHAINS, GIFT WRAP, STATIONERY SEE FIXTURE MANAGER

STORE FIXTURES FOR SALE!

THIS LOCATION ONLY!
HOLLYWOOD & HIGHLAND CENTER
6801 HOLLYWOOD BLVD.
(CORNER OF HOLLYWOOD & HIGHLAND)

EVERYTHING MUST GO!

MONDAY–SUNDAY 10AM–10PM

WE ACCEPT VISA, MASTERCARD, AMERICAN EXPRESS, DISCOVER • NO CHECKS • ALL SALES FINAL • NO RETURNS • NO ADJUSTMENTS TO PRIOR PURCHASES
NO V.I.P. POINTS ISSUED • NO HOLDS • ADVERTISED DISCOUNTS VALID AT HOLLYWOOD & HIGHLAND LOCATION ONLY • SELECTION LIMITED TO STOCK ON HAND

The richly stocked interior of Amoeba Music, located at Sunset and Cahuenga in L.A.

Virgin Records in the heart of Hollywood went out of business with a liquidation sale in June 2009.

Virgin Megastores had been an attempt to enhance the concept of a full-service music store by adding a café and a disc jockey back-announcing songs to promote impulse buying of music. Each store offered an enormous selection of DVDs, books, and magazines to make it a single destination for the entertainment consumer.

But toward the end of the run, the two final Virgins in Southern California barely resembled music stores. A West Hollywood store, which closed in January 2008, was dominated by DVDs; the Hollywood outpost, situated in a stretch of T-shirt and trinket shops, was geared toward tourists more interested in lunchboxes, items with "Hollywood" logos, and pop kitsch than in the Rolling Stones' music catalog. It did not look like a store that specialized in music.

"Like so many others, we have become a lifestyle boutique with toys, books, posters, drinks, and a lot of DVDs," said John Timmons of Ear X-tacy in Louisville, Kentucky. "I have told people numerous times if you ever walk in here and you don't realize you're in a record store, we're done. It's 90 percent music and 10 percent that's helping the bottom line."

> "For the first few years I said hello to every customer. I bought used like a fiend, I hung my own poster collection. Didn't return a CD for four years. We built the store in an honest way."
>
> —PAUL EPSTEIN, TWIST & SHOUT, DENVER

The Lure and the Loss

People who remain in the business of selling recorded music consistently repeat that observation. They recognize that the heyday is gone—when the record store was a gathering place for people who flocked to hear the latest releases, looked forward to getting the advice of clerks, and hung around folks who bonded over songs and artists.

Good record stores had a magical atmosphere. The early ones—those in the late 1930s and '40s, such as Commodore in New York, were thin and cramped. In the 1970s, they kept getting bigger and bigger and the owners bragged about their size and selection; Tower Records in Los Angeles would advertise itself as "the largest record store in the known world." And when they became too large, the smaller places in the funkier neighborhoods defined cool.

Storeowners put their personalities and tastes on the line when they opened their doors. Fundamentally every store was the same: bins with alphabetized LPs, CDs, and tapes arranged by category with featured items at the end of a rack. The lighting was usually too bright and the dust level potent. The personality of a store was determined by the art on the walls, the handful of obscure artists promoted with displays, the music on the sound system, and, of course, the attitude and knowledge of the sales clerks. Even in a generic mall, there would be differences between record stores, much more so than between clothing emporiums.

Once "hip" record stores became staples of communities across the country—generally in the early 1970s—music fans became fanatical about their stores. It could be price, service, the fact that a shop offered used records, a better-than-average stock in a particular genre, or the hours it kept. Allegiances were formed. When teenage shoppers grew up to be record store employees and eventually owners, many reached back to their initial experiences for inspiration. And rather than tap into the modern world, young people who go into the business in the 21st century often base their vision on tales from their parents and older relatives about what made record stores great in the 1960s, '70s, and '80s.

The 1940s through the end of the '90s produced many tales of friends who shopped together, hung out at the local record shop, and, eventually, went on to make music their profession—either as performers or in the industry itself.

In the early 1960s, Bill Bentley went record shopping with Billy Gibbons of ZZ Top in high school in Texas. "You have to find people who want to stay as long you do and I don't think I ever met a woman who wanted to stay in a record store as long as I did," Bentley said. During his tenure as a publicist with Warner Bros. Records in the '80s and the '90s, Bentley shopped with Lou Reed and Costello, who he pronounced "the biggest record store freak I have ever met."

Henry Rollins, the singer, poet, disc jockey, and former frontman of the punk band Black Flag, noted that stories about the importance of record stores in people's lives are not unique. "That being said," he pointed out, "I think there's something really cool about this story that can be told by people living in different countries over decades.

"One of the many great things about music is that it brings people together. Music is such a shared experience. I believe in its great power for good. I don't believe in a higher power but I do think that music is mankind's greatest achievement. Einstein was cool, but he's got nothing on Coltrane."

"I spent a summer in Italy going to every record store . . . searching for a 45 of 'Questa Volta' by the Yardbirds. I was the kid who was invited to parties because I had the records."

—BOB MERLIS,
MUSIC INDUSTRY EXECUTIVE

CAMERON CROWE ON RECORD STORES

Cameron Crowe—filmmaker, journalist, and owner of the record label Vinyl Films—reached back into his childhood spent in San Diego, California, and the desert town of Indio, to create the film *Almost Famous*. He reflected on the meaning of record stores in his upbringing, living in a home where rock music was largely banned and records had to be snuck in.

"Record stores are a community of shared passion. You see the look in people's eyes and you know they're like you; everybody was there for the same reason. The music just sounds better. And you feel like you are in the beating heart of the thing that you love. They are more personal than radio.

"As they start to disappear, you are forced into living rooms and other places to be with your fellow music lovers and hash it out. The record store was a place of escape. It was a library and a clubhouse.

"That's probably why you get people talking about *their* music store, *their* record store because it made your personal journey with music even more personal. That is why [Penny Lane's] line ('if you ever get lonely go to the record store and visit your friends') is in *Almost Famous*. I did feel that those records in that store are your friends and I really miss that," Crowe observes.

"The thing I miss most of all is the stuff that you buy and take home that you would not have bought if you were not at that store at that time. You always hear stuff and you always mixed and matched with your own favorites. In the not-so-distant past, the record store was the validation of music you loved.

"To travel to L.A. to check out Licorice Pizza was a huge thing, and Tower, of course, was great. There was a place in Ocean Beach in San Diego that was instrumental in defining my taste, right next to the Strand Theater where we filmed the opening scene of *Almost Famous*. It was amazing. They had no shades on the windows and the sun would be blazing into this store filled with vinyl, and nobody ever said 'Isn't this going to warp the records?' It never came up. And for some reason the records I got there were never warped.

"They put a copy of Joni Mitchell *Blue* in the window and within about a week, it was Joni Mitchell *Beige*. The place was harshly affected by the sun. It was filled with the smell of incense and had very heavy characters with very heavy musical tastes. Zappa. Neil Young was one of the guys they'd talk about. They'd have bootlegs off in the corner and they'd show it to you if you were meant to understand it. For me, that was a birthplace of great music.

"There was another place in the Brockton Arcade in Riverside near where my grandparents lived. I had my store and my sister had hers. That was my sister's record store. It was the import snob store: The packages were completely expensive and the clerks would hoard the stuff and only play it for you selectively.

"When *Led Zeppelin II* arrived, it was such an event that they put the speakers outside and blasted the entire record out into this little arcade. 'Whole Lotta Love'? I don't know that it has ever sounded better. It just was an elixir.

"It was always the personal touch that made every store different. The record store is the big hand of someone you trust, giving you suggestions and being a facilitator into this private thing. I love the whole experience."

Cameron Crowe (fourth from right), Nancy Wilson (leaning on desk in front of Crowe), and the crew at Grimeys celebrated the release of *Elizabethtown* in 2005.

Tower Records closed its famous Sunset Strip location in late 2006.

Reclaiming the Record Store

The world of record stores started to read its own obituary in early October 2006 when Tower Records announced it would be closing its 89 stores across the country. In New York, the clerks reported that customers offered condolences and spoke in solemn tones during the store's last month. The feeling was that a close friend had died.

In many cities across the country, Tower was the gold standard. It had the deepest selection, sales floors that would feature the entire catalogs of many artists, in-store appearances and signings by the biggest stars, and it developed a rock-hard brand loyalty with its customers. Eventually it expanded too far overseas, borrowed too heavily, and could not recover.

Tower's founder Russ Solomon walked away from the business—but only for a short while. He returned in 2008 with R5, a 6,000 square foot independent ("indie") store in Sacramento that he says "is the resurrection of our original San Francisco store."

The concentration is on new CDs, LPs, and 45s, "pretty ordinary if there is such a thing," he said. He noted that the change in retail between 2003 and 2009 was one of the most dramatic periods he had seen in his 60 years in the business.

Men and women actively working in retail music frequently compliment Solomon, often describing him as a visionary.

Competing with Tower after it became a dominant chain never troubled many in the industry. That likely owes to the belief that Tower put music first and hired clerks who were devotees. Creating a store that could vie with Tower was an honest challenge that many store owners accepted in the 1970s, '80s and '90s.

Neil Schield grew up in the digital age, but longed for the atmosphere of Tower. In April 2009, he opened a 400-square foot store called Origami Vinyl in Los Angeles' Silver Lake district to sell new vinyl only. The target audience is hipsters attracted to the nearby live music venues, coffeehouses, bars, and the building where Elliot Smith's *Figure 8* album cover was shot.

"What's really cool is when older people come in here and say they have not seen a record store like this since they were in college in the '70s," Schield said.

Even though he did not experience record stores during their peak—Schield was born in 1976—he is among those who crave the romance of that era.

> ## "Record stores are cool."
> **—STEVEN VAN ZANDT, E STREET BAND, ACTOR, RADIO PERSONALITY**

Counterculture Commercialism

In an ironic twist, one of the least commercially successful musical ventures of the 1960s—the Woodstock Arts and Music Festival held in August 1969—would have a significant impact on the 1970s. The Monterey International Pop Festival, held in 1967, ushered in an era of major labels signing rock acts by the dozens; Woodstock showed the executives who made up the audience for this music, and also its size. It proved to be the flashpoint for marketing: Music for older adults was pushed to the back burner as record labels had a new target—youth, and a new approach.

"The record store era," explained Jim Greenwood, the founder of the Licorice Pizza chain in Southern California, "was when you promoted the song on the radio *and* in the record store. That lasted from, like, '69 to the late '70s when all those other influences took hold. Philosophically, there was something about the art of the LP that led people to make (buying decisions) based on the visual. Looking at the cover and saying 'wow this looks cool' was an important part of that era."

"Working in a retail store was not something you took lightly," said Hale Milgrim, who created a record department in his father's toy store in 1960 and ascended to the presidency of Capitol Records three decades later. "It isn't quite *High Fidelity* whereby the customer better like what I like and if you don't, then you're wrong. I was taught there was music out there for everybody.

"Any time I had control of the turntable while on the floor of the store, I would look where people were mingling and play music by bands in that section. I wanted to create or add to the conversations."

The Early Years of Buying Records

For anyone whose first music purchase predated MTV in its mid-'80s glory years, the exercise likely began at a local department store, drugstore, or electronics shop. The purchase was one 45 rpm record or, if they were in a bargain rack wrapped in plastic, three 45s for a buck. This would continue at a shop accessible on foot or bicycle until a car became available. The 45s would give way to LPs; department stores would eventually be skipped over for bona fide record stores. The decades are different for various individuals, but the anecdotes bear remarkable similarities.

Keith McCarthy started buying records in 1965, obsessively collecting one particular style for a few years, then moving to another—jazz, then electric blues, then acoustic blues, avant-garde jazz, power-pop and punk, and so on. His only job in a record store was his first one, at the Manhattan E.J. Korvette's on Fifth Avenue between 47th and 48th Street.

"This was going to be great," McCarthy thought, "because I could get any album at cost—99 cents. I would spend my entire paycheck there and take home about 120 records every week."

He was hired in June 1969, the day after school let out, and fired about two months later. "I lied and said I was at a friend's house but I went to Woodstock. One of the guys I worked with told my mother. I didn't get fired because I lied, but because of all the news reports about the drugs and they thought there were orgies and crazy hippies. They thought I was one of those people."

His second job was again strictly to feed the record-buying habit—but at retail prices. He worked weekends at United Press International as a copy boy. "I would make about $100, $120, and go across the street to this store at 43rd and Third," McCarthy recalled. "It was run by these two jazz fiends. They turned me on to Charlie Parker, then Sonny Rollins and John Coltrane. I'd go home with a pile of records and about $10."

A suburban New Jersey guy like Doug Herzog, the MTV executive who signed the agreement to refer to Michael Jackson as The King of Pop, had a trail that many others would ride in the 1960s and '70s: The singles were bought at the local Korvette's; a visit to New York during his teen years meant a stop at Sam Goody's and Disc-O-Mat; and once in college—in his case Boston—record stores were everywhere. Once you find that record nobody else seems to have, it's obvious you have been bitten by the bug. For Herzog, it was an import copy of *Bob Marley and the Wailers Live*.

Marc Weinstein, a co-owner of Amoeba Music in Los Angeles, San Francisco, and Berkeley, grew up outside of Buffalo. The Record Boutique in Kenmore, New York, was where he

Jim Greenwood, owner of the Licorice Pizza chain in Southern California, chats with Michael Jackson at a "meet and greet" in 1974.

shopped in junior high and high school. "The owner, Don, used to hip us to all the upcoming releases. So we'd pool all our money on Tuesdays to buy something we were all dying to hear."

After that it was road trips to Toronto to visit Sam, the Record Man, and A & A Records or House of Guitars in Rochester, N.Y. "That was music-geek heaven in the '70s— an absolute mass of records and instruments. LPs piled in every nook and cranny. We used to make that pilgrimage as often as possible. I found all the Heldon LPs there for 2.99 each."

Joe Brauner, who would eventually become a talent agent, graduated from the chain stores to an independent shop called The Record Baron in Staten Island, N.Y., in the mid-1970s.

The people who ran the store would "invite me and my then-high school girlfriend to their homes to listen to new albums, drink lots of Boone's Farm [wine], and smoke copious amounts of pot. We were 17 and the whole thing was crazy, but it revolved around discovering new music and albums. The day that Bruce Springsteen's *Darkness on the Edge of Town* was released was 'an event'!

That album cover—and Bob Seger's *Night Moves* and Aerosmith's *Rock* and every new release by my favorite band, the Good Rats—those really take me back."

Step back for a second to the idea of the 45s. In the 1950s and '60s, it was common practice for stores to allow customers to listen to records before purchasing them. In big cities, listening booths were standard at any good record store.

In 1982, when original owner Louis Karp, and later, partner John Kunz, were crafting the design of Waterloo Records in Austin, Texas, their model was "the stores of old."

"A place where you could hang out and take a stack of 45s and go into a booth to listen," Kunz said. He noted that the purchase of a shrink-wrap machine was one of the store's smartest moves: It allowed him to open a record, let a customer listen to it, and then wrap it again. "It's all about putting the music first. Everyone told us that letting people listen would put us out of business in a week. We wanted a place that would attract musicians, artists, writers, tastemakers. Could we meet their needs?

"I believe that letting people listen to music and a return policy whereby you can return anything and exchange it are things that set us apart to this day."

Kunz is one record store owner who speaks with a lilt of hope in his voice. Many longtime owners do not have that. You can hear frustration. You can hear indecision. You definitely hear nostalgia. But there is also determination.

New York's Downtown Music Gallery left its longtime street-level home on the Bowery in March 2009 for a basement level shop in Chinatown. Discussing the subject with co-owner Manny Maris requires patience; talking about this move, for him, requires an understanding of Manhattan real estate, commute times, the infrastructure of Internet commerce, and why the Constitution needs revamping.

"People are not going to stumble over us on a back street in Chinatown the way they did before," Maris said. "I'm going to miss the person who comes in and asks 'Do you have the new Madonna?' and, after fighting the temptation to lock them out, turn them on to something they have never heard. The thrill for me is still having a living room where I can put something on to knock somebody's socks off. We're going to continue to serve people that way."

The selection at Waterloo Records in Austin, Texas, has attracted hundreds of musicians, artists, and writers.

A BUMPER STICKER BUILDS A BRAND

Every record store needs a logo. Some work out better than others.

When John Timmons was opening his store in Louisville, Kentucky, he considered a number of names, among them the rather plain John's Records. He did not consider bumper stickers, even though they would eventually become a crucial part of the store.

He wanted to pay tribute to his favorite band, the British pop-rockers XTC, and came up with Ear XTC. "I thought I might get sued by the band," he recalls.

"I sat at my typewriter and changed the spelling phonetically and worked on it." Once he came up with the spelling, he needed to create a logo. "I have no artistic ability. I looked at the Cheap Trick logo and used the typewriter font and kept enlarging it. About a year after I opened the store, there was a pesky salesman who wanted to sell me stupid shit. He kept coming back, offering me all kinds of things I didn't want and I said 'I give in. What's the cheapest thing you have?' It was a bumper sticker.

"I hate bumper stickers, and I can't believe people put bumper stickers on their cars. But it took off and became a popular item.

"Flash forward six years. The Gin Blossoms (from Tempe, Arizona) come to the store and the lead singer Robin Wilson put a bumper sticker in his mouth during a photo session. They changed the booklet in *New Miserable Experience* and put that picture in it.

"Billboard did a story on the store because of the bumper sticker. Then Cameron Crowe came here to shoot *Elizabethtown*. He would be in here buying records almost every day, bringing the cast in. He says, 'I'm going to do something for you, show Ear X-tacy some love.' The bumper sticker is on a wall in a scene and it's on camera for a good five or six seconds."

MTV came to Louisville to cover the premiere and Kurt Loder did an hour-long interview with the stars in the store. Orlando Bloom went on *Oprah* and talked about the store, offering her a Timmons creation—a "Keep Louisville Weird" T-shirt.

"I always see artists wearing our shirts but then Rhett Miller of the Old 97's walks in here wearing a Waterloo T-shirt," Timmons laughed. "That logo has been good to us."

Collectors and Sellers

Every good record store in America today probably has a collector behind it. Amoeba's Weinstein is a Sun Ra fanatic with 250 of the jazz pianist/bandleader's albums in his personal collection. One of his business partners, John, is obsessive for Louis Armstrong. Doyle Davis at Nashville's Grimey's buys up soul, jazz, and funk. Bob Koester, whose Delmark label and Jazz Record Mart in Chicago would have instrumental roles in the history of electric blues and free jazz, initially focused on his primary interest—78s of traditional jazz from New Orleans prior to World War II.

"How do you straddle daily business with your collector sensibility? Half your employees are not collectors and some are not even music people," said Paul Epstein who never worked in a record store until he owned Twist & Shout in Denver in the mid-1980s. "It was a dream—a juvenile dream—but somewhere I transitioned and became a serious business man."

Village Music's John Goddard was a blues fiend. "First of all I was a music fan, then a collector, and third, a businessman."

Before he started Dusty Groove in Chicago, Rick Wojcik was a graduate student with, as he calls it, "the sickness." That meant spending non-study hours combing through record stores, flea markets, and thrift shops in the hunt for old jazz, R&B, Brazilian, and funk albums.

"For years and years, if I found something I already had, I would not buy, figuring somebody would want it. Then I started to think maybe I am doing a disservice by leaving that record in a small store in Baltimore."

Hale Milgrim's Santa Barbara home is a reflection of his 25 years in the record business—first at Discount Records, then Warner Music's distribution arm WEA, the Warner Bros. label, Elektra Records, Capitol—and the concert promotions he has done since 1994. "I'm a collector who's like a kid any time I enter a good record store," Milgrim said while standing inside his shrine to musicians and bands from a multitude of eras. Autographed guitars and the painting that served as the cover of Richard Thompson's *Rumor and Sigh* stand out among the myriad of promotional items within the music-oriented spaces in his home.

Photographs, backstage passes, cardboard cutouts, and other items associated with The Grateful Dead and The Beatles far outpace any other act; there's a Peter Gabriel sledgehammer, a puzzle for Talking Heads' *More Songs About Buildings and Food*, a Fleetwood Mac *Rumours* tambourine, Juluka sweatbands, and a Jesse Winchester football for his *Third Down and 110 to Go*. Milgrim's office is wall after wall of well-organized CDs and LPs along with decades of Grateful Dead live tapes organized chronologically in drawers.

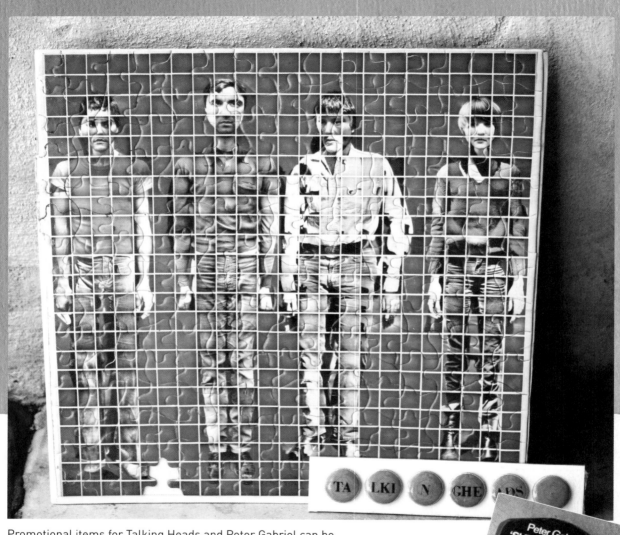

Promotional items for Talking Heads and Peter Gabriel can be found in Hale Milgrim's personal collection.

Capitol Records' president Hale Milgrim presented Paul and Linda McCartney with RIAA sales awards for *Off The Ground* and *All The Best* in 1993.

THE UNTOUCHABLES

Three items in the collection of Village Music's John Goddard that he will never sell or trade:

A 16" by 20" high school graduation portrait of Janis Joplin

A gold record for Columbia/Legacy's *Robert Johnson: The Complete Recordings*, the only one presented to a record store

Billie Holiday's passport

Lenny Kaye, who defined psychedelic garage rock with the groundbreaking compilation *Nuggets: Original Artyfacts from the First Psychedelic Era, 1965-68*, saw a social universe form at Village Oldies in New York City when he started working there in 1970.

"There's a vast fraternity of record collectors, and the record store was their hub. There was not a lot of information on these groups or the labels so you'd gather [there] and it would be like a library. I gravitated toward group harmony records because that's who I would see singing on the sidewalk.

"I always go to a local shop because it's a gathering place. I also enjoy the museums of the world. They're places where you can browse at will," Kaye concludes.

Home Sweet Record Store

When John Goddard opened Village Music in 1969 in Mill Valley, California, he was bored with the standard promotional posters advertising new albums. Already a fan and collector, he was so entrenched in records and memorabilia that each time he rented an apartment, he got a two-bedroom unit specifically to use one of the rooms for his record collection. The room would be decorated—walls, ceiling, doors—with posters and photographs.

"I started bringing stuff from my home into the store and decorating the store with my personal collection," he said. "What happened was that people would come to the counter with their records and see something on the wall or on a counter and it would prompt them to ask if I would be interested in buying something they had. In some cases, people would give me things they were tired of that I was thrilled to get."

From the early '70s until he closed the store in 2007, every surface was covered in art, whether old record covers, publicity stills, posters, or nearly life-size cutouts of film stars from the '40s and '50s. It was truly a visual paradise for any fan of the soul music of the 1950s and '60s that Goddard relished.

"One day a guy walks into the store and says he used to fetch Cokes for (early rock 'n' roll DJ) Alan Freed. He had letters to Annette Funicello, a snapshot of Lavern Baker lifting up Buddy Holly,

John Goddard, pictured in 1990, used his personal memorabilia collection to give Village Music in Mill Valley, California, its unique look.

eight or nine programs from the shows at the Paramount in Brooklyn (that Freed produced). He gave me a price that was 10 percent of what I would have offered him."

For 30 years, John was not willing to part with anything. At some point in the early 1990s, a buyer from the Hard Rock Café looked around the store and announced that he was interested in four of Goddard's posters, unaware of the owner's pack-rat mentality.

"I said no to his offer. He says 'I'm talking serious money.' I repeated myself and said 'no thank you.'

He says, 'I don't think you understand. I'm with the Hard Rock Cafe.' And I rejected the offer again. He turned red and stormed out of the store."

John changed his philosophy sometime around 2001 or '02. "I couldn't rationalize that if someone is offering $5,000 for a poster that I ripped off a telephone pole, I should take it. Something about the record collector in me met the real world. Do I need 125 John Lee Hooker albums or can I get by with 25 really good ones? Once you start [purging], it gets easier."

Decorating a store can also give fans something to talk about when they meet one of their idols. Peter Jesperson was a Beatlemaniac; he identifies his first day of work at Oar Folkjokeopus in Minneapolis not just by the date, but by the fact that it was the day Paul McCartney's *Red Rose Speedway* was released.

Jesperson, whose career included managing the Replacements and creating Twin/Tone Records in the late 1970s, decided to have the store get behind the 1974 release by McCartney's brother Mike McGear. Simply titled *McGear*, McCartney co-wrote the songs and produced the album; McCartney, wife Linda, and Wings members Denny Laine, Jimmy McCullough, and Denny Seiwell performed on the album. Jesperson had Warner Bros. send the store 100 empty jackets to make a wall display, the album sat in the new releases rack for a year and it ultimately sold 475 copies. That sort of effort only arose when a fan who wanted

the public to connect with his or her taste was working behind the store's counter.

In 1989, Capitol Records had a promotional event for McCartney's *Flowers in the Dirt* and through a roundabout way, Jesperson secured an invite. "Paul surprised everyone and shows up. I got to say hello and I started to mention the *McGear* story and he became so enthralled. We went into a corner and had good 10-minute conversation uninterrupted. It's one of my favorite things to ever happen to me in the record business."

Naturally, not everyone starts out at a record store as an enthusiastic collector. There are exceptions like Terry Currier of Music Millennium in Portland, Oregon. When he got his first job in a record store—in 1972—he was a clarinetist who neither owned albums nor listened to the radio much. In his first month on the job, he turned down free Pink Floyd concert tickets. He started to date a girl who worked at another music store and one evening, for a post-work surprise, she took him to Music Millennium, which stayed open an hour later than his own employer.

The bug got him: During his senior year in high school he purchased 665 albums. He was still playing the clarinet while also exploring the saxophone and oboe. The school counselor called him into the office to get him to fill out applications for scholarships, which he refused.

His response? "I was assistant manager of a record store making $2.25 an hour and I'm only a

Oar Folkjokeopus in Minneapolis, shown in 1977, was named for two of the owner's favorite records: *Oar* by Skip Spence and *Folkjokeopus* by Roy Harper.

senior in high school. It doesn't get any better than this." These days you can still find Terry behind the counter of Music Millenium. He took over from founder Don McLeod in the '80s and went on to win many record retail awards over the years.

Making a Difference

If not for random incidents in record stores far from the centers of the music industry, the members of R.E.M. might have never met, the Police and Buena Vista Social Club might have not landed early pockets of popularity, My Morning Jacket might not have broken out of the Louisville scene, and Matt Groening of *The Simpsons* would not have found a place to distribute his first comic, "Life in Hell."

"I met Matt when he was a $2.50-an-hour clerk at the Licorice Pizza store across the street from the Whisky a Go Go," said Peter Case, who would go on to lead the Plimsouls and have a fruitful solo career. "I traded a copy of the first album by my band, the Nerves, for the first copy of 'Life in Hell.'"

There might not be a more famous band that traces it roots to a record store than R.E.M. Michael Stipe was a customer at Wuxtry, the store where guitarist Peter Buck worked, and the two struck up a friendship based on mutual tastes.

"He came into the store a lot and was into Suicide, whatever was current at that point," Buck remembered. "We did have the same kind of taste and he was interested in records because of the covers. He was also buying weird jazz."

Stipe, Buck said, was one of the few musicians he has worked with who never had any retail job. Bertis Downs, who later became R.E.M.'s manager, was fresh out of law school when he stopped into Wuxtry to purchase a Neil Young album and, as a result, forged a friendship with Buck.

"If you want to be in the music business but you don't know how to get in, it's the first place you start," Buck said.

R.E.M. lore became so crucial to the city of Athens, Georgia, that, in late 2007, the Athens Historical Society presented a symposium titled "R.E.M. in Perspective." Included were films of the band practicing in the Atlanta Wuxtry store.

Nearly two decades later, a customer from New York asked the clerk behind the counter at Ear X-tacy in Louisville, Kentucky, for something local that he might not know about. A few months after that, store owner Timmons recounted, "Mike Martinovich is managing My Morning Jacket and taking them to a new level."

Before John Kunz partnered with original owner Louis Karp at Waterloo Records, he successfully pitched the owners of the mainstream chain, Disc Records, on the idea of a hipper outlet. From that pitch arose Zebra Records in Austin, which specialized in imports and items that would be more likely to sell based on their "cool" factor. While there, Kunz would get his first taste of being an integral part of the chain that links bands and fans.

"My assistant manager is playing (the Police's) 'Roxanne' and he took it down to KLBJ. [The Police] did an in-store signing here that was great, And they played the Armadillo World Headquarters that was overflowing. They were playing a lot of places that were half full. The Austin crowd wouldn't let them go. They came back for a second encore and third encore and finally said 'we don't know any more songs.' The crowd wouldn't leave so they played five or six songs they had already played."

The members of My Morning Jacket, regulars at Ear X-tacy in their hometown of Louisville, Kentucky, are pictured playing to a very appreciative crowd in 2008.

Years later, Waterloo was the first store in the country to report that *Buena Vista Social Club* was its No. 1 seller. That claim could also be made for other future smash hits such as Norah Jones' debut, the soundtrack to *O Brother, Where Art Thou?* and Los Lonely Boys' debut. "I couldn't be prouder of those four records," Kunz said.

Vicki Hamilton became a management consultant for Motley Crue after befriending lead singer Nikki Sixx at the Licorice Pizza where Groening had worked. The band's manager had hired her to put up displays of the Crue's album *Too Fast For Love*. "I stapled my finger to Vince Neil's face which Nikki thought was 'killer.' Those were some fun, outrageously wild times."

Village Music's Goddard announced his closing

CAREER WEEK SUCCESS STORY

During his junior year of high school in Wilmington, Delaware, Other Music co-owner Chris Vanderloo went to the local record store to offer his services, for free for a week. "He said all right, and I put in my week, and had to write a report about it. About two weeks after I finished, he called up and said he would hire me. 'I'll pay you this time.' I am probably the only person who ended up working in the business chosen for Career Week."

nine months before locking up one last time. In the early spring, a tour bus parked out front. "B.B. King had driven from Las Vegas to see the store one last time. He spent a lot of money and did wonders for my ego. I'm thinking 'this is B.B. King.' He doesn't get through a concert without sitting for a good portion of it and here he's standing on his feet shopping for almost five hours. You can't measure moments like that."

Fighting the Stereotype

From the middle of the 1990s to the early part of the 21st century, record stores lost a bit of their luster. Chains had expanded on the strength of pop, rap, country, and soundtracks, not to mention the boy band explosion, which sent plenty of old-time fans scurrying for a new place to hang out.

It produced a record store type, most vibrantly reflected in the film *High Fidelity*, in which John Cusack plays a record obsessive, Jack Black is pretentious and surly to the nth degree, and Todd Louiso portrays the introspective geek with great taste.

It's comical in hindsight to hear record store owners say they did everything possible to avoid the Jack Black stereotype.

"We'd have meetings about that," said Steve Bergman of Schoolkids in Ann Arbor, Michigan. "We were happy to see customers and we had to be able to sell a Journey record without making the customer feel like a jerk."

When the spoof newspaper *Onion* reported "37 Record-Store Clerks Feared Dead in Yo La Tengo Concert Disaster" in 2002, they completely tapped into the record store Zeitgeist. They set the story in Athens, mentioning the 40 Watt club and Wuxtry by name. Among the missing, they reported seven freelance critics, five vinyl junkies, two fanzine publishers, and a college radio DJ.

The indie store was a daunting place. Just ask Homer Simpson. The finale of the seventh season of *The Simpsons* (not-so-coincidentally created by Matt Groening) found Homer venturing into a record store and immediately going into an emotional funk over his inability to recognize the names of the bands on the racks. Homer equates his ignorance with a loss of cool, never mind his outrage when his children know nothing about

Grand Funk Railroad, and, worse, they can't stand the band's music.

That episode debuted in 1996 when chains and mom & pop stores were healthy.

"Record stores need to be community places," Kimber Lanning of Stinkweeds in Phoenix said. "People who don't know music and walk into my store become wide-eyed. Too many of them don't know this music because it is not being played on the radio."

Lanning was among the independents who felt the need to make record stores part of the bigger whole, playing a role in not just the business of record music but also community development, small business associations, and the performing arts.

She opened a performance space in 1999 called Modified Arts and operated it as a non-profit to support touring bands and local acts. Arcade Fire, Bright Eyes, Blonde Redhead, and Red House Painters are among the acts that performed there early on.

Advocacy for the independent music world picked up steam around 2005, eventually resulting in the first Record Store Day in 2008.

Stars were called upon to offer comments on what makes record stores, especially indies, so important.

John Mellencamp proffered: "Immersing yourself in the environment of a real record store where music is celebrated and cherished adds real

"The museum element of stores stimulates people."

—RAND FOSTER, FINGERPRINTS, LONG BEACH, CALIFORNIA

value to the experience of buying music. In some ways, that retail experience is as important as the music."

Jack White has not only opened a Third Man Records in Nashville, he has used "pop-up stores"—storefronts that are rented for a few days—to promote his records with the White Stripes and Dead Weather. White stated that it is "high time the mentors, big brothers, big sisters, parents, guardians, and neighborhood ne'er-do-wells start taking younger people that look up to them to a real record store and show them what an important part of life music really is."

Bruce Springsteen revealed his spending habits. "I'll go into a record store and just buy $500 worth of CDs. I am single-handedly supporting what's left of the record business."

Some may wonder exactly where the Boss is buying those compact discs. The good news is that hands are going up across the country. There's a

37 RECORD-STORE CLERKS FEARED DEAD IN YO LA TENGO CONCERT DISASTER

APRIL 10, 2002

ATHENS, GA—Thirty-seven record-store clerks are missing and feared dead in the aftermath of a partial roof collapse during a Yo La Tengo concert Monday.

"We're trying our best to rescue these clerks, but, realistically, there's not a lot of hope," said emergency worker Len Guzman, standing outside the 40 Watt Club, where the tragedy occurred. "These people are simply not in the physical condition to survive this sort of trauma. It's just a twisted mass of black-frame glasses and ironic Girl Scouts T-shirts in there."

Also believed to be among the missing are seven freelance rock critics, five vinyl junkies, two 'zine publishers, an art-school dropout, and a college-radio DJ.

The collapse occurred approximately 30 minutes into the Hoboken, NJ, band's set, when a poorly installed rooftop heating-and-cooling unit came loose and crashed through the roof, bringing several massive steel beams down with it.

Andy Ringler, an assistant manager at Wuxtry Records, sustained head trauma when he ran back into the building to rescue a fellow clerk.

"I just had to help," said Ringler, listed in stable condition at a nearby hospital. "I saw all these people coming out bleeding and dazed. I gave up my vintage Galaxie 500 shirt just to help some guy bandage his arm. It was horrible."

Added Ringler: "I just pray they can somehow get this club rebuilt in time for next month's Dismemberment Plan/Death Cab For Cutie show. That's a fantastic double bill."

Joe Gaer was among the lucky record-store clerks who escaped unscathed.

"I was in the bathroom when it happened," said Gaer, a part-time cashier at School Kids Records. "There was this loud crashing sound, followed by even louder crashing, and then all these screams. If I hadn't left to take a leak during 'Moby Octopad'—to be honest, never one of my favorite songs on *I Can Hear The Heart Beating As One*— I'd probably be among the dead."

"It's just tragic," Gaer continued. "I heard they were going to play Daniel Johnston's 'Speeding Motorcycle.' They almost never do that one live."

Devastated by the disaster, Athens record-store owners are still holding out hope that their employees are still alive.

"All I can do is wait and pray they'll find them," said Bert's Discount Records owner Bert Halyard, who lost clerks Todd Fischer and Dan Harris in the collapse. "They were going to start an experimental/math-rock band together. Dan had a really nice Moog synthesizer and an original pressing of the first Squirrel Bait EP."

As of press time, police and emergency rescue workers were still sifting through the wreckage for copies of Magnet, heated debates over the definition of emo, and other signs of record-store-clerk life.

"I haven't seen this much senseless hipster carnage since the Great Sebadoh Fire Of '93," said rescue worker Larry Kolterman, finding a green-and-gold suede Puma sneaker in the rubble. "It's such a shame that all those bastions of indie-rock geekitude had to go in their prime. Their cries of 'sellout' have been forever silenced."

Jack White created special "pop-up" stores that would open for less than a week to promote his albums with the White Stripes and Dead Weather.

visceral reaction to the virtual worlds and the lack of physical, tactile information.

While a student at the University of Michigan from 2004 to 2007, Matt Kivel, a California native and co-leader of the band Princeton, found the record store atmosphere there "so refreshing." One store, PJ's, located on a second floor above a Subway sandwich shop, stood out. "The owner, Mark Tara, and the other guys changed my perspective just by talking to me at length. It was old school pontification—I felt like I was going to preparatory school for record buying. I would give him music I was making and they'd play it in the store. It was the first place that sold any of my band's stuff. It was a nurturing environment."

The Mooney Suzuki's Sammy James Jr. is among those who agree with the sentiment. For Record Store Day he said: "rock 'n' roll needs to be seen, touched, smelled, and tasted just as much as heard. I want to unroll the poster, open the gatefold, explore the cover art and the liner notes."

"Records are interactive and so, too, are stores," said author and former Warner Bros. Records executive Bob Merlis. "You go with one thing in

mind and return with alternatives whether you got input from sales people or you're trying to intuit the quality of a record."

People who have bounced around various jobs or once held positions at record labels echo the thought of Mike Dreese, who opened Newbury Comics in Boston in 1979 after dropping out of M.I.T. "Going into the record store business was a way to rebel against the idea of mainstream career."

The history of contemporary music, particularly in the rock 'n' roll era, has used album releases as its timeline with only the occasional live performance inserted as a landmark—the Beatles on *Ed Sullivan,* Bob Dylan plugs in at the Newport Folk Festival, Jimi Hendrix and Otis Redding at Monterey Pop, the Sex Pistols in San Francisco. The record stores, by and large, were the conduit, the clerks and owners who cared about the music playing the role of tastemakers and having as significant an influence as many critics. Musicians, oddly enough, split into two camps: Students who wanted to have as large a collection and hear as much as possible, and those who heard music and were inspired to create. The former set worked in record stores; the latter group got jobs in guitar shops.

In chronicling the evolution of record stores, it's a bit astonishing how often history repeats itself. The creation of vinyl-only stores in the early 21st century neatly parallels the creation of LP-only stores 50 to 60 years earlier. The number of owners who were employees and then bought the store they worked in continues to this day. Many stores started as racks in electronic-repair shops. And an astonishing number of record labels began in stores—this dates back to the 1920s and has fascinating chapters in every decade.

Del Bryant, the president of the performing rights organization BMI, who has worked in music publishing since the late 1960s, noted, "The great small stores were never occupying prime real estate, but everybody knew where they were. You'd drive behind the malls or down an alley to find them. There were always small—about 500 or 1,000 square feet."

There's a lure that burns eternal.

John Brenes got his first record store jobs in 1959, working at three of them at once. He bought records from all over the city of Los Angeles, which made him seek out a fourth paying gig. "I had to get a job as a busboy at an Italian restaurant to pay my tab at record stores."

Drafted into the Army, he served in Vietnam and returned home to a much-different L.A. First he moved to the northern California town of Petaluma, opening the Music Coop and moving it four times in the city before relocating the store to Ashland, Oregon.

"When I was 24, I wanted a record store," he said, "and I still have the attitude that I own the candy store and can eat when I want. Maybe [my wife and I] clear $12 an hour but I've had the store for 35 years. Every single day that I've had this job I can't wait to get to work. That has a value you can't put a dollar sign on.

"I think back on the songs on those first albums I bought. The records were more important than any girl, even if the song was about a girl. The girl was gone but the song remained."

Record shops have thrived because one generation after another has been addicted to that experience. It is easy to romanticize. Record stores were places where friendships and romances began, where bands formed, where information was shared, and where people enjoyed parting with significant portions of their paychecks.

The experience of those of us who shopped in record stores, owned them, or worked in them varies across the U.S. and from the beginning of the 20th century to the 21st. However, the love for sharing music ties us all together. Cue up a CD or LP while we take a trip from the inception of the record store to its rebirth.

IT'S CALLED WHAT?

Where did those store names come from?

Tower Records. The store, which opened in 1960, was first a part of the Tower Drug Store in Sacramento, California.

Licorice Pizza. Folk duo Bud & Travis had a routine on a live album about how to use their unsold copies of an earlier album: sprinkle sunflower seeds on it and make a licorice pizza.

Oar Folkjokeopus. The Minneapolis store was named after two of the owner's favorite albums: *Oar* by Skip Spence of Moby Grape and the Jefferson Airplane, and *Folkjokeopus* by Roy Harper.

Criminal Records. Eric Levin opened Secret Service Records in Daytona Beach, Florida. After being in business for three months, he was arrested on an arcane law that makes it an offense to call a business the Secret Service. "There were so many cops down there that the news crews came and covered it," Levin said. On TV that night, a newscaster joked around after the story was aired, "What will he call it now? Criminal Records?" Levin stayed in Florida for another year before moving to Atlanta where Criminal Records went into business in 1991.

Rhino Records. Owner Richard Foos said "We spent hours with a group of people saying names, whatever they thought of. And when someone said Rhino, I said 'that's it.'"

CHAPTER 2

KINGS OF SWING

A MUSIC FAN accustomed to the fine offerings at San Francisco's music shops passes by Wiley B. Allen, a seller of pianos, and is taken aback by the window display. Rather than pitching a baby grand, this 1924 window dressing is dedicated to a new record by Al Jolson: "California, Here I Come."

The display includes images of the Pacific Ocean and an imaginary golden gate, a reference to the song's lyrics. Ahead of its competitors, the Wiley B. Allen store installed record players with earphones that allowed customers to play a record before buying one.

San Francisco and the Bay Area were ahead of most of the country, outside of New York City, when it came to recorded music.

With World War II on America's mind, Wallichs Music City, Commodore, and Sam Goody invent a business from scratch

> "The focus of the energy in a record store cannot be replicated on the Web."
>
> —LENNY KAYE, MUSICIAN

The OKeh label mostly released R&B records but it also issued the occasional country record.

Pressing plants in Oakland kept the stores well stocked, but since each store only carried selected labels, an avid music fan had to travel from store to store to stay current. Wiley B. Allen, for example, carried Brunswick releases. A blues fan looking for a new Mamie Smith record had to head over to Walter S. Gray's shop, which exclusively carried the OKeh label. Back in 1917, Sherman, Clay & Co. had become the exclusive Victor distributor, making it the place to go to get the latest in Victrolas.

The display idea caught on. As shoppers browsed the area, the come-ons were as wide-ranging as the music—a pop singer like Eddie Cantor in one window, a bust of Beethoven in the next, pictures of Duke Ellington after that. Records were by no means cheap in the 1920s. An album of classical 78s ran about $7—the average salary was about $100 a month—and individual 78s ran between 65 cents and a dollar. The Five & Dime stores, however, were serviced by another collection of labels that brought prices down to below 50 cents a disk. While the radio brought live music and other entertainment into living rooms, the Victrola and other record players gave listeners the opportunity to choose what they heard. Music, for the first time ever, was physical.

Records, pressed on shellac and played at 78 rpm, were sold for more than 30 years before anyone decided a store could operate solely on disk sales.

Records could be found just about anywhere and were often sold in conjunction with the machines used to play them. At the turn of the 20th century, even Bloomingdales had a record department selling, in 1905, disks for the prices determined by Victor and Columbia—$1 for a 12-inch record, 60 cents for the common 10-incher, and 35 cents for a 7-inch record.

Records were stocked on warehouse shelves in the earliest music stores, such as this one, photographed in 1905.

In 1906, there were 25,000 record dealers, a total that would be cut to 7,500 fifty years later, and to below 3,000 a half-century after that. To generate sales of 78s and sheet music, shops would host the equivalent of in-store performances: songwriters such as Jerome Kern and Irving Berlin would perform their songs off the backs of trucks, and Tin Pan Alley song pluggers would play tunes on pianos in New York beach towns or at the local Woolworth's or McCrory's.

Up through the late 1920s, radio, music publishing, and records were three distinct industries that saw each other as a threat. The three businesses tried a joint experiment in late 1926 by having a sheet music publisher pony up $30,000 to hire bands while stocking dealers with sheet music for songs that would be played in special radio shows across the country. The logic was that music fans would flock to get the sheet music the next day. The program bombed.

The Tony Zender music store, New York City,
in the very early 20th century

Victor Dog on Every Record

If you don't get the dog, you can't
get the best results.

For sale everywhere—25,000 dealers.

Records were
popular items
to carry from
the get-go; this
1903 ad indicates
Victor discs
were available at
25,000 stores.

Record companies had little sense of precisely
what would sell, and throughout the country,
regional labels would crop up for specific
marketplaces. Decca, Columbia, and RCA Victor
were the East Coast majors up through the 1940s,
but even they were willing to try various regional
musical forms.

Victor & Edison stores, such as this one photographed in 1908, sold audio equipment as well as 78s.

First World War I and then the Great Depression made the companies experiment with different ways to get as much music released as possible. A standard method was to give performers a flat fee for their work rather than offer contracts with royalty payments based on sales. The effect, decades later, was that a considerable amount of American music was captured for posterity. In some cases, the source was rather odd.

Take the Wisconsin Chair Co. in the Midwest. Based in Port Washington, Wisconsin, the company produced phonograph cabinets for the Edison Co. beginning at the turn of the 20th century. The company started making records in

> "78 collectors like holding a piece of history. The 78 collectors who talked to me when I was 13 made me feel like we were rubbing shoulders with history. We went to wild places."
>
> —DAVE ALVIN, MUSICIAN

As shown in this 1921 newspaper ad, demonstration and listening rooms introduced the public to recorded sound.

Decca was one of the major labels in the first half of the 20th century.

Blues legend Charley Patton recorded songs such as "High Water Everywhere" for Paramount Records, a label owned by the Wisconsin Chair Co., which built consoles for phonographs.

1917, with music designed to appeal to German, Scandinavian, and Mexican immigrants.

In 1922, it began producing "race records" and would become revered for its recordings by blues greats Charley Patton, Blind Blake, Blind Lemon Jefferson, and Skip James. The records were given away when customers bought furniture. But in many cases it was up to the musicians to get their records sold. In the liner notes to the Revenant Record box set *Screamin' and Hollerin' the Blues*, it is noted that Patton had some of his strongest sales at picnics.

Musicians of the period opened record stores—one of the prime ones was the Sunshine Record Co.

Ansell, Bishop & Turner used Victrolas to attract customers in Washington, D.C., in 1921.

For years after the Victrola was introduced, most of the sales occurred around the holiday season. This ad is from 1922.

The JUNE Victor Records are here

Victrolas

THIS IS OUR MUSIC WEEK SPECIAL ONLY **65.**

THE VICTOR EXPOSITION

VICTOR RECORDS

Victrola

Now is the time to select your Victrola for Christmas

Victrola Instruments and Victor Records are so much in demand for gifts that there is a shortage every Christmas. Place your order now while all the twenty-one instrument styles at from $25 up and complete record stocks are available.

Ask your dealer or write to us for illustrated catalogs.

Victrola
Victor Talking Machine Company, Camden, N.J.

Victor Records in **German**

Victor Records in **Bohemian Hungarian Russian Polish Hebrew**

Companies like Victor produced foreign-language records to entice immigrants.

THE OLDEST RECORD STORE IN THE U.S.

George's Song Shop in Johnstown, Pennsylvania, holds the title of the oldest existing record store in the United States. It was founded in 1932 by Bernie George, though his brother Eugene took over four years later and willed it to his son John in 1962.

"I saw an article in *Billboard* in 1992 that said National Record Mart, at the time a chain in Pittsburgh, was the oldest chain in the States. It started in 1939," John George said. "That got me thinking we could be the oldest. So we started asking distributors about their oldest accounts and searching on the Internet, and the closest we came was a store that had been operated by a lady in Seattle that opened in 1935."

George's Song Shop, about 70 miles east of Pittsburgh, has had six locations—it has been at its current spot since 1977—and has twice lost its inventory to floods (1936 and 1977). Stocked with about one million 45s, 50,000 LPs, and 20,000 CDs, one key to the store's endurance has been its continual stocking of multiple formats. Over the years, the owners have bought about 25 warehouses of records and CDs when distributors and stores have gone out of business.

The store is floor-to-ceiling music, a place

George's Song Shop has been in business since 1932 in Johnstown, Pennsylvania.

store run by brothers Johnny and Benjamin "Reb" Spikes. They opened their shop in Los Angeles' South Central district in 1919 and it quickly became the hub for the city's black musicians, according to Steve Isoardi's liner notes for the Rhino Records' set *Central Avenue Sounds*. It was the only place in Los Angeles where records by black musicians could be purchased.

The brothers also opened the Dreamland Cafe, where musicians would hang out as well. They owned, too, an after-hours joint in Watts called the Wayside Park Cafe where New Orleans trombonist Kid Ory led his Creole Jazz Band. Johnny, a drummer, and Benjamin "Reb," a pianist, ran their own Majors & Minors Orchestra, and, as composers, wrote "Someday Sweetheart," a hit for Alberta Hunter, and the lyrics to Jelly Roll Morton's "Wolverine Blues."

Records by Ma Rainey and Mamie Smith did well at the store and after selling 100 copies of Hunter's "Someday Sweetheart," they decided to create their own label. In 1922, at a studio in Santa Monica, they recorded Kid Ory's Creole Jazz Band, marking the first time a New Orleans jazz band was ever recorded.

Among other musicians to go into music retail was jazz pianist Clarence Williams, the second most recorded black artist in his day, who went into business in 1919, two years after starting a music publishing company.

Prior to becoming "the mayor of Central Avenue," drummer Curtis Mosby, a native of Kansas City, Missouri, opened a record store in Oakland, California, in 1921.

Jazz and blues were not the only rivals to crooners, opera stars, and show tunes.

Songs about Kentucky Folk hero Floyd Collins were favorites in the mid-1920s.

Singer Ruth Etting was one of Columbia's featured artists in the late 1920s.

"Don't Let Your Deal Go Down Blues," by Charley Poole and the North Carolina Ramblers, was the first country music hit, released in 1927.

What would eventually come to be called country music had a moment in 1926 that was denigrated by the entertainment industry trade publication *Variety* in a front-page story.

"For the local dealer," *Variety* wrote on December 29, 1926, "the hill-billy craze spells a bonanza. The ignoramuses buy as many as 15 records at a time, often of the same title. If one wears out they have a back up." "The Prisoner's Song" and "Floyd Collins" were two major hits purchased by "the illiterate and ignorant" swayed by "the sing-song nasal twanging vocals."

Charley Poole and the North Carolina Ramblers had the first certifiable country music mega-hit in 1927 when "Don't Let Your Deal Go Down Blues" sold 102,000 copies. The flip side of the Columbia release was the rural-minded "Can I Sleep in Your Barn Tonight Mister." A later Poole record, "The Girl I Loved in Tennessee," sold 65,000 copies.

Throughout the Great Depression, the price of sheet music was constantly lowered, eventually hitting a dime after being as high as a quarter. Records went for 15 cents at newsstands and, in 1930, the major labels were able to sell 500,000 records a week. Brunswick's stars were the band of Ben Bernie, singer Al Jolson, and jazz trumpeter Red Nichols; Columbia had Ted Lewis' band, singer Ruth Etting, and the Charleston Chasers; and Victor's roster included Rudy Vallee, Maurice Chevalier, and Duke Ellington. In 1940, drummer Gene Krupa came up with the gimmick of releasing 24 records in 25 weeks; this did not yield any hits.

Drummer Gene Krupa signs an autograph at George's Song Shop in Johnstown, Pennsylvania, in 1941.

As Americans crawled out from under the Great Depression, record sales boomed. In 1939, Americans bought 58 million records. A year later, the tally went to 70 million. Some of that owed to price-slashing as pop records went for 50 cents, a quarter less than the price in 1939, and records on discount labels such as Bluebird and Varsity were selling for 35 cents.

Models for the Modern Day

Four stores became models of the modern-day record store: Commodore, Colony, and Sam Goody's in New York, and Wallichs Music City in Los Angeles. Two of those stores were responsible for two of music's most important record labels: Commodore, the first independent jazz label, and Capitol Records, which was founded by the owner of Wallichs Music City. Colony was the hub of activity in midtown Manhattan; Sam Goody's pioneered the sales of LPs.

"When the LP came along, he opened an LP-only store," Tower Records founder Russ Solomon said of Sam Goody, a tinge of awe affecting his voice. "At his 49th Street store, he decided that if you bought $25 worth of LPs—and they're going for $4.85 apiece—he would give you a player. He only broke even on each first purchase, but he had made a customer.

"The LP was perfect for classical. He was able to build a business by going to record companies

Philip L. Newman, a retired anthropologist, would step back in time whenever he visited the Jazz Man Record Shop in Los Angeles in the 1960s.

"You walked into the Jazz Man and saw 78 records stacked along the walls and in bins down the center of the store," Newman recalled. "In the back, there was a little counter and Don Brown [the owner] would usually be back there, puffing away on a cigar. The floors were wooden and creaky and the records were kind of dusty.

"But it was all there. If you wanted Louis Armstrong's 'Potato Head Blues,' he would have multiple copies at different prices, depending on the condition—some were pretty scratched up and some were in good shape."

Eventually the store moved to Santa Monica and on Saturdays the store would host get-togethers for fans to listen to 78s, drink beer, and argue about music. It lasted until the store closed its doors in 1983.

The Jazz Man Record Shop in Los Angeles specialized in New Orleans-style jazz, swing, blues, and some jug bands.

and telling them, 'If you remaster these recordings and issue them on LP, we will buy enough to pay for it.' Theirs was the only store to do multi-million dollars in sales. He convinced the majors, Columbia and RCA, and a few independents, to release LPs. What impressed me, as a shopper, was he had enormous selection. He was one interesting guy."

The man who went by the name Sam Goody was born Samuel Gutowitz in 1904. He had a toy store in lower Manhattan and, in 1938, a customer asked if he had any records. Goody found some 78s in his basement and sold them for $25. He went into the used business before becoming the top LP store in the country. The West 49th Street store eventually stocked 38,000 LPs and, in 1955, Goody stores accounted for 7 percent of the total national sales of LPs. It was one of the first record stores to discount prices.

Colony also had a non-musical beginning. Colony Sporting Goods went out of business at Broadway and West 52nd Street in 1948, prompting Harold S. "Nappy" Grossbardt and

Sidney Turk to open Colony Records. Like Commodore, its location gave it a specific customer base: musicians, theatergoers, and nightclub patrons. Frank Sinatra, John Lennon, and Michael Jackson shopped there on occasion.

Grossbardt created two offshoots, Nappy's and Tin Pan Alley, in the 1950s and 1960s, and worked at Colony until 1988. It moved to the Brill Building in 1970 and built a reputation for catering to the Broadway crowd.

Milt Gabler and His Red Hot Commodore

Like the other shops, the Commodore store was converted to sell records. As a teenager, Milt Gabler worked first at his father's hardware store on East 42nd Street across from Grand Central Terminal and then at the Commodore Radio Corp., a popular radio and speaker supply store that his father also owned. A fan of "hot jazz," he placed a speaker above the doorway to attract customers by playing the radio.

Customers would enter the store and ask if it sold records. After a few times of telling them no, Gabler persuaded his father to let him stock records, specifically jazz 78s. Soon the records were outselling radios and, in 1934, the store's name was changed to the Commodore Music Shop. Commodore and Sam Goody's were similarly

Sam Goody's Manhattan location, shown in the late 1960s

shaped—only about 10 feet wide and about 40 feet deep—and extremely cluttered.

Gabler would also buy out-of-print jazz recordings. The majors had no interest in reissuing them so Gabler started Commodore Records to press new versions of older records; Commodore was the first reissue label in the country. It was also the first to print all of the names of the musicians on the record labels.

And in 1938, Gabler expanded Commodore to include new recordings. His first session was with Eddie Condon, a guitarist who was a regular in the store. A couple of Commodore regulars, Alfred Lion and Francis Wolf, would start Blue Note Records a year later.

Since so many people hung out in the store, Gabler knew he had a story worthy of press coverage. Commodore fan Frank Norris wrote

A classical recording on Milt Gabler's Commodore label

Milt Gabler (fifth from left) along with Jack Crystal (Billy Crystal's father, far left), Louis Armstrong (fourth from left), store employees, and record collectors at the Commodore Record Shop in New York City, 1947

about the store and the label in *Time*; Alexander King had *Life* do a photo essay; and Gabler was profiled in *The New Yorker* in 1946 when the word "hot" was slang for jazz.

The New Yorker reported that he had sold more hot records than any other music-shop proprietor. "He has manufactured, under the Commodore label, some of the world's best hot recordings, and he has made them fashionable at the not inconsiderable price of a dollar and a half a copy," *The New Yorker* article stated.

High Fidelity magazine called the store "the country's most important source of 78's and a meeting ground for fans and musicians." Norris reported in *Time* that Commodore was more than a record shop: It "provides loafing room for most of the city's hot musicians."

With a jazz society associated with the store to boost sales, the Commodore store's backroom also had a mimeograph machine to produce *Jazz Information*, a fanzine that listed Ralph Gleason among its editors.

Gabler, whose story was told by his nephew, Billy Crystal, in the one-man Broadway show *700 Sundays*, also created a mail order company, the United Hot Record Club of America. At its peak, it trailed only Sears, Roebuck and Co. and Montgomery Ward. Commodore Music Shop closed in 1958.

"I Found a New Baby" Out West: Wallichs Builds an Empire

Glenn Wallichs made a living selling and repairing radios until he sold his five shops to open a record store at Sunset and Vine in Los Angeles in 1940. Nat King Cole and his trio performed at the opening. Located across the street from NBC, it was an immediate success and attracted a steady stream of celebrity customers—Bob Hope, Bette Davis, Rudy Vallee, Jack Benny, Rita Hayworth.

The largest music emporium on the West Coast, within a year it became the city's most popular place to purchase records, radios, instruments, and sheet music. It also had custom-recording facilities.

"One part of the appeal of Wallichs was the listening booths," said Richard Foos, founder of the Rhino Records store and label. The booths allowed customers to listen to records before

Actors Natalie Wood and Bobby Driscoll were among the celebrities who shopped at Wallichs Music City in the heart of Hollywood in 1953.

buying them. "They had a really big selection, their own (top-sellers list), which was real cool, and sheet music. The negative, as a young rock 'n' roll fan, was that everything was list price. They also catered to older clientele."

COLLECTORS BENEFIT FROM THE FIRST CHAIN IN THE U.S.

Pittsburgh, Pennsylvania has long been hailed as one of the best collectors' markets in the country. In 2005, a reporter for the *Pittsburgh City Paper* was at a disco in England and stumbled upon a British DJ who would travel to the Iron City two or three times a year looking for vintage soul music. It turns out American-music vinyl junkies were more keen on Pittsburgh and western Pennsylvania than on any other city.

Jerry Weber, owner of the all-used, all-vinyl emporium Jerry's Records, attributes the city's supply to one record store from the past, National Record Mart, the first music-store chain in the United States.

"They made an outstanding effort to special order anything, no matter what it was," said Weber, who made the transition from record collector to storeowner in 1976. "Ethnic music, pop music, blues. Since the early 1950s, this was a great big pocket for record stores and every town had its own National Record Mart. It was a great depository."

National Record Mart began when Hyman Shapiro and his sons Sam and Howard opened their first music store in 1937. A tiny storefront in downtown Pittsburgh, they called it Jitterbug Records and sold used jukebox records for a dime apiece.

Intriguingly, Weber's son Will has a specialty shop within Jerry's Records called Whistlin' Willie's 78s. It carries about 25,000 78s. While the records of the 1940s and '50s are often a dime a dozen, Weber said "there's always a market for pre-war records of the '20s and '30s—no matter what they are."

National Record Mart started selling new records and had added two other stores by 1941. Hyman's youngest son, Jason, eventually joined the business. Frank Fischer was hired in 1951 to wash windows and floors; he would eventually become president of the operation. By the 1960s, the chain had 20 stores and started moving into malls.

When *Pittsburgh City Paper* printed its list of prime shops, it mentioned five places, only two of which were open regularly in 2009: Jerry's Records and Attic Records. Record-Rama had received some media attention after its owner Paul Mawhinney attempted to auction on eBay its collection of 3 million records in 2008.

A $3 million winning bid proved fraudulent and Mawhinney remained determined to sell the collection as a single entity. After the auction failed, he changed the name to Record Rama Sound Archives and would only sell duplicate copies of records.

Wallichs' first significant problem came from the Big Three—RCA, Columbia, and Decca would not sell him records directly, forcing him to buy those records from another distributor. At the same time, he wanted to expand his custom recording service, which was used for audition disks, air checks, and personal messages.

One of his steady customers was Johnny Mercer, the songwriter, who had branched into film production as well. They bonded after Mercer's wife Ginger had surprised the songwriter by getting a radio installed in his car in 1935 when Wallichs was doing that type of work.

Wallichs, Mercer, and Paramount production chief Buddy DeSylva sat down and decided to create a record label. Mercer would put up most of the money and Wallichs would run the label. DeSylva would be its chairman. They considered the names Liberty and Victory—this was in 1942, with the U.S. at war—but both were dropped for being too similar to old company names. They went with Ginger's suggestion: Capitol.

Wallichs was widely credited as the driving force behind the success of the label, which was housed in offices above the record store until the famous Capitol Tower was built in 1956.

Amoeba Music is a tip of the hat to Wallichs.

"From day one," said Amoeba Music co-owner Marc Weinstein, "we wanted to be in the tradition of Wallichs Music City. That held such a place in people's hearts. It took a year to find but the whole reason to be (at Sunset and Cahuenga) was to be in the same neighborhood as the original Wallichs."

Capitol had neither a factory nor a distribution system, and the shellac that was used to make 78s was being rationed. Wallichs got records manufactured and set up a distribution system with offices in 24 cities. It was the first major label based on the West Coast.

The label's first release came in June 1942—Paul Whiteman's New Yorker Hotel Orchestra performing "The General Jumped at Dawn" b/w "I Found a New Baby."

Fifteen days after Capitol started, the American Federation of Musicians was able to secure a ban on recordings, claiming that records killed off job opportunities for musicians. Imagine starting a

brewery a month before prohibition started. The ban would last for a year. Wallichs, which would open two satellite stores that were nearly as large at the flagship, was two bus rides away from Cary Mansfield's home. Mansfield was a regular customer in the 1960s and eventually managed the store for three years until a year before it closed in 1977. "We'd go into Hollywood once a month to shop for records and Wallichs would always be saved for last," said Mansfield, whose souvenirs from the store include bags, sheet music for "Hooray for Hollywood" that he would have stars sign when they shopped there, and even a brick from the building, rescued from the rubble when the store was torn down. "It was the premier store."

Wallichs was also the first store to sell used albums as it unloaded the demonstration records that customers would take into listening booths. By the time they were put on sale for 99 cents, they would be pretty scratched.

Listening booths, according to Philip L. Newman, a retired anthropologist, "were real hangouts for the kids" during his high school years in the late 1940s in Eugene, Oregon. "That was very exciting. You'd talk at lunchtime about what kind of things you'd listen to when you went down to the booth."

Composer William Bolcom was a fan of the listening booth; he used them growing up in Seattle in the 1940s. And he sees their value today, a thought he expressed for National Record Store Day in April 2009.

"I am of the generation where one could still go into a booth at the record store to listen before deciding to buy. In this way I first became acquainted with Stravinsky's recording of 'The Rite of Spring' as well as John Kirkpatrick's landmark recording of Ives' 'Concord Sonata.' Both were overwhelming experiences for me and would form a great part of my musical universe.

"For me the ideal store would revive the listening booths. . . . I know that downloading and streaming are the musical dissemination modes of the future, but maybe if young people would be made aware of what is lost by just hooking up with music on the iPod . . . it could revolutionize musical taste."

A CENTURY OF FORMATS

As the style of music has changed over the last hundred-plus years, so has the format of how it is recorded and distributed.

Edison wax cylinder. Thomas Edison patented the tin-foil cylinder phonograph, intended as an office dictation machine, in 1877. Columbia Records began making commercial recordings in 1890. By 1897, three companies—Edison, Berliner-Johnson, and Columbia—were selling 500,000 cylinders annually.

The very first phonograph played cylinders.

78s. Introduced in 1901, the Victor Talking Machine Co. opened to manufacture flat disks that had been pioneered by Emil Berliner. A year later, Columbia and Victor standardized the formats at 7 inches and 10 inches. Double-sided disks were introduced in 1904. The Victrola, which became the most popular device to play the disks, was unveiled in 1915.

LPs. The long-playing album, made of plastic, appeared in 1948. Columbia spent four years developing the 12-inch "long player" that rotates at 33⅓ rpm, and had early hits with cast albums of *Finian's Rainbow* and *Kiss Me Kate*. In 1958, RCA and Columbia issued the first stereo recordings.

"Style D" of one of the first phonographs, c. 1915

45s. RCA introduced the 7-inch single in 1949. A year later, Capitol was the only label issuing records in all three speeds (78, 45, and 33⅓). At first, cautious labels would issue records as 78s and, if they sold well, would issue them as 45s. Once rock 'n' roll took hold of the singles marketplace in the late 1950s, their durability made them the format of choice for teenagers.

Reel-to-reel. With its roots in Germany in the 1930s, the format was developed in the late 1940s by American audio engineer Jack Mullin.

A CENTURY OF FORMATS

After World War II, Mullin developed the system with the hope that film studios would use magnetic tape for movie soundtrack recording. Bing Crosby ponied up $50,000 for Ampex, becoming the first performer to master his recordings on tape and pre-record his radio shows. RCA Victor introduced pre-recorded reel-to-reel tapes in 1954 and the format was popular with audiophiles in the early '70s.

2-Tracks. Also known as PlayTapes, the system was created by Frank Stanton in the 1940s while he was in the Navy, and introduced for use with music in 1966 to compete with 4-track cartridges. Sears, which sold a player for $19.95, and MGM Records, which had a deluxe model that went for an extra 10 bucks, got behind the PlayTape, pitching it as a replacement to the transistor radio. Stanton foresaw the expansion of the PlayTape as a recordable format for dictation and home hi-fi systems, neither of which came to pass. The downfall of the format came when the players were not installed in cars.

4-Tracks. Earl Muntz was the first to attempt to manufacture and market the 4-track tape, which had been around since 1956 and largely dismissed. Muntz licensed music from major record labels and marketed players and prerecorded tapes. The 4-track cartridge had two programs—an A side and a B side, essentially—and offered better sound quality than an 8-track. What Muntz did not anticipate was the involvement of a car company in the development of a tape player.

8-Tracks. William Lear, designer of the Lear Jet, invented the 8-track stereo and patented several car radios. The format was designed for use in cars and developed by the Ampex Magnetic Tape Co., Lear Jet Co., and RCA Records. Ford Motors was the first to offer 8-track players as an option, debuting them in their 1966 line. Labels stopped making 8-track tapes between 1981 and '83, although mail-order record clubs continued to offer them deep into the 1980s.

Cassettes. Philips Co. invented the cassette tape in 1962. Its use did not become widespread until the 1970s. Once the Sony Walkman was introduced in the U.S. in 1980, cassette sales picked up considerably, eventually hitting 500 million units sold in the mid-1980s. As the industry sought to fade out vinyl 45s, the "cassingle" was introduced. Once CDs caught on, interest in cassettes dwindled and once mix CDs could be made on computers, cassettes nearly became extinct.

Compact Discs. Sony and Philips created the first compact discs in 1982—this marked a milestone shift from analog to digital storage and playback of audio—and started selling players in the U.S. a year later. This remains

the dominant over-the-counter format to this day. Enhancements of the CD, the MiniDisc, Dual Discs, and the Super Audio CD failed to capture the general public's fancy. Sony released the first CD player on October 1, 1982 in Japan and, with it, the first CD, Billy Joel's *52nd Street*.

MP3s. The Fraunhofer Institut in Germany received a patent for MP3 digital file storage in 1989 and a U.S. patent in 1996. Winamp, a Windows application, was the first successful computer program that could play an MP3; it was introduced in 1998. In February 1999, the Seattle label SubPop became the first to distribute music tracks in the format. That same year, portable players were introduced.

CHAPTER 3

SHAKIN' ALL OVER

THE FIRST MAJOR all-country music record store opened in May 1947 at 720 Commerce St. in downtown Nashville. Ernest Tubb opened his self-named Ernest Tubb Record Shop and would develop a strong regional following by broadcasting live music in a Midnite Jamboree immediately after the Grand Ole Opry on Saturday nights.

Tubb's shop was the original listening center in Nashville. "If anybody wanted to know how a new 78 sounded, they'd take it out of the package and crank it up loud on the old Victrola. You could hear it all over," Will Jones, a manager of one of the six Ernest Tubb Record Shops, told *Billboard* in October 1995.

LPs and 45s change listening habits in the 1950s as Elvis Presley turns the world on its ear

On most Saturday nights, the hub of country music had three-stops—the Ryman Auditorium for the Grand Ole Opry, Tootsie's for a few drinks, and then on to Ernest Tubb's, where the Midnite Jamboree was staged in the back of the store.

"Ernest Tubb's was right across the street from Tootsie's (honky tonk)," said Del Bryant, president and CEO of BMI, and son of songwriters Felice and Boudleaux Bryant, who penned many a hit for The Everly Brothers. "My parents would get us down to Tubb's real quick after the Opry and sit us on the risers next to the stage. Many a night was spent looking at those cowboy boots keeping time. It was so completely packed. The whole west end would close down. I doubt anybody could have bought a record then, it was so crowded in the store."

Tubb, known for "I'm Walking the Floor Over You" and "Soldier's Last Letter," had attempted a mail-order operation for two years that never turned a profit. Opening a shop was driven by complaints from fans who could never find his records in stores. In the 1950s, the store moved down the block, which brought it closer to Tootsie's Orchid Lounge and the Ryman.

In 2009, the store is as much a tribute to Tubb

The Midnite Jamboree at Ernest Tubb Record Shop became a significant country music event.

and the honky-tonk music he performed as it is a shop to get the latest country releases. Box sets dedicated to the country stars of the '40s, '50s, and '60s are prominently placed toward the front register, a re-creation of the Midnight Jamboree stage is in the back, and an array of fading photographs of old stars fills the walls. If someone ventured in and knew nothing about Tubb, they would leave realizing he had the words "thank you" painted on the back of his acoustic guitar, which he would turn toward the audience as a response to their applause.

To hold the Midnite Jamboree, record racks were pushed to the side of the store until the late-night broadcast moved to a theater in 1974. The only show that has run longer than the Midnite Jamboree is the Opry. The Jamboree was strictly a showcase for young hopefuls and their latest record releases, and it usually only booked two guests each time.

Patsy Cline, whose signature is painted on the roof of the Ryman, appeared at a 1953 Jamboree and, over the next 40-plus years, remained the store's biggest-selling female artist. Elvis Presley, rejected by the Grand Ole Opry, received Tubb's invitation to perform on the Jamboree in 1954 and, to this day, Presley souvenirs and albums remain on the downtown store's shelves.

Tubb's show was a rare union of radio and record purveyor—the two industries had been at war with one another due to a second ban (in 1948) on the manufacturing of records championed by the American Federation of Musicians, which contended that recordings took jobs away from musicians who played on radio shows.

While record sales dropped that year—150 million disks vs. 265 million in 1947—two labels were able to embellish their standing in the industry. One, Columbia, did it with technology. The other, the brand new Capitol, did it with stars.

Much of the success of Columbia Records owed to its introduction of the long-playing 33⅓ album. Columbia was able to get customers on board with the new format through a tie-in with Philco, the electronics company, which offered a $29.95 attachment that allowed 33⅓ rpm albums to be played on Victrolas. The label also had major hits with *Finian's Rainbow* and *Kiss Me Kate*, two of the first Broadway cast albums to be released as long-playing records.

But if the year belonged to anyone, it was Capitol Records, the label housed in offices above Wallichs Music City at Hollywood & Vine. Peggy Lee's "Mañana," Nat Cole's "Nature Boy," Margaret Whiting's "Tree in the Meadow," and Pee Wee

The Ernest Tubb Record Shop was the first record store to only sell country & western music.

Hunt's "12th Street Rag" had made Capitol the first major player on the West Coast. Newsweek estimated "Mañana" sold 1.5 million copies.

Capitol released 405 singles and 44 albums in 1948, and became the first label to send promotional copies to radio disc jockeys. It was also the first full year that Glenn Wallichs held the title of president of Capitol Records, succeeding his partners songwriter Johnny Mercer, who left the presidency to work on songwriting projects, and film producer Buddy DeSylva, whose health was failing.

Lyons & Healy, Chicago, Illinois, c. 1945 (from the Record Retailing Yearbook)

Wright's demonstration room, Kansas City, Missouri, c. 1945 (from the Record Retailing Yearbook)

Gramaphone Shop, Wilkes Barre, Pennsylvania, c. 1945 (from the Record Retailing Yearbook)

Store Owners Get Jazzed

Glenn Wallichs's idea that a record store would be a proper birthing place for a record label started to take hold. Many a jazz label got its start in record stores in the 1940s.

Tempo Records in Los Angeles gave birth to Dial in 1946 and would release albums by Charlie Parker, Dexter Gordon, Teddy Edwards, and Howard McGhee. The Session label came out of the Session Record Shop in Chicago in 1943 and had blues hits with Mama Yancey.

Bob Weinstock was 16 when he started a mail-order operation in his family's apartment, wholesaling jazz reissues to stores in New York. He then opened the Jazz Record Corner on West 47th Street. In 1949, when he was 20, he launched New Jazz and, soon thereafter, Prestige, which he ran until 1971.

Only 11 companies were listed in the original LP guide, but by 1955 there was a massive proliferation of labels attracted to the business for a variety of reasons. One of the more prominent technical changes was the switch to vinyl from a shellac base to make records, adding to their durability and reducing the weight. The introduction of magnetic recording tape allowed mixing and editing various takes of a piece of music with no discernable loss of sound quality.

Between 1948 and 1950, labels waged a speed war. Columbia was behind the creation of 33⅓ LP;

TABULATING THE HITS

In addition to film grosses and Broadway ticket sales, *Variety* tracked the sales of sheet music, jukebox records, and disks at retail from the 1900s into the 1960s.

The Top 10 in the 1940s was created by polling individual stores in 10 cities: Davegas Stores in New York, Hudson-Ross in Chicago, Denel's Music Shop in Los Angeles, Sherman-Clay in Seattle, and Jenkins Music Co. in Kansas City, Missouri, among others.

The week prior to Christmas 1948, Dinah Shore's "Buttons and Bows" was No. 1 nationally and No. 1 in four cities. The No. 2 record, "My Two Front Teeth," by Spike Jones, was No. 1 in five cities but it did not chart in three.

RCA Victor was the driving force behind the 45. Capitol was fine with 78s until 1952. The labels were changing shapes and sizes of records at a startling rate.

"I went into Columbia Records (sales department) and they had all of these 10-inch LPs for $1.90 each," said Bob Koester, who was restocking his Jazz Record Mart. "The next night, I open the newspaper and there's an ad for a department store: All Columbia 10 inches half price—$1.49.

"I returned to complain. They say 'didn't you get

> "The dumbest thing to do is name a label after a store. Does your competition want to advertise your store?"
>
> —BOB KOESTER, OWNER OF DELMARK RECORDS AND JAZZ RECORD MART

Writing in the Jan. 5, 1949 *Variety*, columnist Bernie Woods opined "to place three or four songs on one side of a 10-inch disk is too risky. Even if two become hits, and the second and third turn up toes, the sale potentiality is badly reduced."

Elvis Shakes Up the World

In early 1956, David Budge's mother returned home from her job as a publicist for RCA Records and told her son she had a surprise for him. His excitement was tempered by the fact that he had already purchased a 45 of Elvis Presley's "Hound Dog" with "Don't Be Cruel" on the flip side. It was the only record he owned. Sheepishly, he told his mother he already owned the Elvis record.

"Pick a hand," she insisted. David played along.

"And she holds out the first album," said Budge, son of tennis champion Don Budge, whose celebrity friends included Frank Sinatra, Bing Crosby, and Count Basie. "The only albums I had seen were in my dad's jazz collection and my mom's show tunes. I never considered the possibility of rock 'n' roll being on a big 33⅓ album."

Presley shook up the music world in 1956, not just in his domination of the various charts, but in terms of ushering in a new era for record stores.

"Heartbreak Hotel" was Presley's first hit, sitting at No. 1 for seven weeks on *Billboard*'s Top 100

our letter?' No, I always bought C.O.D." They lowered the price on 10-inch LPs to a dollar apiece for Koester.

"But how do you have an industry give up on a format like that? The 10-inch LP was standard for jazz and opera. Riverside had 125 10-inch LPs, Folkway had 1,000 titles. Blue Note was all 10 inches. The majors didn't distinguish between jazz and pop," meaning that jazz listeners who had become accustomed to the 10-inch album were about to get something new, a 12-inch LP.

The 10-inch LP was ostensibly a forerunner to the Extended Play or EP that caught on in England but never in the U.S. At the time it was introduced—the late 1940s—the record and radio industries still had issues with one another and were almost a decade away from getting into bed together.

starting April 21. It was the most played song on jukeboxes for eight weeks, the biggest sold record at stores for eight weeks, and the song that received the most spins on radio for three weeks. The top radio hit that spring had been "The Poor People of Paris" by Les Baxter; the single that followed Presley's reign was hardly a rock 'n' roller—Gogi Grant's "The Wayward Wind."

"Hound Dog," with "Don't Be Cruel" on the B side, was an even bigger hit. The record sat at No. 1 from August 18 until the end of October, topping the jukebox, bestsellers, and radio charts from September 15 to the end of October. It would be the decade's biggest hit.

"Hound Dog" was the first record that stores could not keep in stock. Bob Merlis, who would co-write a book on black music from 1950 to 1976 called *Heart & Soul*, ventured to HyGrade Electronics in Brooklyn to get either the 78 or the 45.

"I gave them the money and they gave me a piece of paper," which obviously confused a young

Elvis Presley, an avid record buyer, browses the hits at a Memphis record store in 1957.

kid. "They called when it was in, and it was in a bag that was closed and stapled with my name on it. That felt special."

Having three consensus No. 1s—meaning his record held the top slot on all four pop charts—Presley achieved a feat unheard of and then repeated it in 1957 with "All Shook Up," "Teddy Bear," and "Jailhouse Rock."

In 1956, RCA Victor sold 13.5 million records, of which Presley represented 20 percent. Sales of Presley paraphernalia also boomed. On February 23, 1957, *The New York Times* reported that $20 million of Elvis-logo'd fashion items had been sold—jackets, skirts, bracelets, nylon scarves, and so on. Drugstores and novelty shops were selling lipstick in the shades of hound dog orange, love you fuchsia, and heartbreak pink.

The rock craze had caught on in the city: The Paramount Theatre in Times Square set a new box office record when one of Alan Freed's rock 'n' roll revues sold $204,000 worth of tickets over 10 shows.

"Hound Dog" would become the No. 1 single on the R&B chart simultaneously with its run on the pop chart, making Presley the first white artist of the decade to top the R&B chart. *Billboard*, at the time, based its charts on the location of stores and jukeboxes, as well as the target audience of radio stations.

Looking at the No. 1s on the R&B charts from 1956 through 1958 is to witness rock 'n' roll's birth: The El Dorado's "At My Front Door," Little Richard's "Long Tall Sally" and "Rip It Up," and Shirley & Lee's "Let the Good Times Roll" in 1956; Laverne Baker's "Jim Dandy," Chuck Berry's "School Days," and Jerry Lee Lewis's "Whole Lotta Shakin' Goin' On" in 1957; and Danny & the Juniors's "At the Hop," the

Champs's "Tequila," the Elegants's "Little Star" in 1958. Those three years also saw multiple No. 1s from Fats Domino, Sam Cooke, and the Platters. Nearly all of the hits were on independent labels.

Capitol Records was the first major label to respond to the Elvis craze, signing Gene Vincent, who promptly had a Top 10 hit with "Be-Bop-a-Lula." But Columbia, the other major label, was having no part of rock 'n' roll.

"It's not music," Mitch Miller, the head of Columbia's pop music division, famously said. "It's a disease."

Besides, the majors were busy creating global stars without rock 'n' roll. According to a 1956 global overview in *The New York Times* of March 18, London was big on Frank Sinatra and Fats Waller, Louis Armstrong had fans parading in Moscow, and Doris Day was hot in Buenos Aires.

In England, 60 million records were sold; in Germany, 30 million; and Brazil, 15 million, 45 percent of which were LPs. The LP caught on quickly in France, where it cost close to the equivalent of $8 apiece—more than twice the U.S. domestic price, and Australia, where Mario Lanza's *Student Prince* was the biggest seller of '55. Every major city in the Soviet Union had a record-manufacturing factory. Record sales topped 8 million in Argentina with 30 percent of the sales going to tangos.

Elsewhere the assimilation rate was slower. Mexico saw a 30:1 ratio of 78s to LPs; in Argentina

Rockabilly singer Eddie Cochran and his fiancee, songwriter Sharon Sheeley, shop for records at Wallichs in the late 1950s.

it was 13:1. The Japanese were quick to buy hi-fi systems but slow to purchase albums: The average owner of a hi-fi only bought one album every two months. In early 1955, RCA Victor cut the prices of its records by 23 percent to 40 percent in the U.S. All Victor LPs had a list price of $3.98; 10-inch records went for $2.98. It became a bit confusing. Labels would have as many as 20 "list prices" and since not every store was afforded the same wholesale price, an album might cost $4.25 in one store and $5.95 down the street.

Columbia responded by cutting some of its

prices but kept its classical LPs at $4.95 and $5.95. For the first time, according to a *Time* magazine report (January 10, 1955), there were independents fearing they would be run out of business.

Things Ain't the Way They Used to Be

Once rock 'n' roll and R&B gained a foothold in the country, independent labels started sprouting up everywhere, as did record stores that could specialize in music for younger people. Many stores grabbed the opportunity to start a label.

Dot Records was founded by the owners of Randy's Record Shop in Gallatin, Tennessee, and from 1950 to '56, they focused on the gospel and R&B of Jimmy C. Newman, Ivory Joe Hunter, Joe Liggins, and The Counts. Their biggest hitmaker was Pat Boone; one of their most collectible records was Jack Kerouac reading his writing while Steve Allen backed him on piano.

In Harlem, Bobby's Records would be the home of the Robin, Fury, Fire, Flame, Everlast, and Enjoy labels between 1951 and 1962. With a focus on blues and doo-wop, their artist roster included Lightnin Hopkins, Elmore James, Wilbert Harrison, the Shirelles, and Gladys Knight & the Pips.

Cactus Records and the Record Factory in Beaumont, Texas, joined forces in 1952 to create the country label Starday, the first label home for George Jones, Roger Miller, and Dottie West.

One of the legendary record shops in Los Angeles was Dolphin's of Hollywood, an R&B-centric store located in South Central at Vernon and Central Avenue. Though many miles south of the actual Hollywood, he used the name to draw attention to the fact that Jim Crow laws were keeping black people out of parts of Los Angeles.

The store opened in 1948, and in 1951, John Dolphin started recording artists and issuing their records on his four labels: Recorded in Hollywood, Lucky, Cash, and Money. He had hits with the blues singer-songwriter Percy Mayfield, R&B singer Jesse Belvin, jazz saxophonist Illinois Jacquet, and early soul singer Bettye Swann.

The store was open 24 hours a day so that factory workers could shop after their shifts, regardless of what time they got off work. KRKD broadcast from the store, and since the disc jockeys were on the store's payroll, the records on Dolphin's labels received considerably more airplay. However, the station was considered crucial in creating one of the first crossover hits ever: the doo-wop cut "Earth Angel" by the Penguins. With a live DJ, the store's parking lot became a significant

The Holiday Shop in the Roeland Park Shopping Center, Roeland Park, Kansas, was a typical record store of the 1950s.

were stiffed. Future Beach Boy and Hondells member Bruce Johnston and drummer Sandy Nelson were waiting for Dolphin's arrival at his office on the night of Feb. 1, 1958, along with shipping clerk Percy Ivy, who had submitted four songs to Dolphin but had never been paid.

When Dolphin arrived, Ivy started arguing with him, pulled a gun, and fatally shot him five or six times. The store, run by Dolphin's widow Ruth and Rudy Ray Moore, remained open until 1970.

party scene, attracting crowds of hundreds on Saturday nights. Since KRKD played black music that appealed to white listeners, crowds were often racially mixed at the store.

The list of legendary performers who made appearances at the store to greet fans is staggering: Billie Holiday, Little Richard, James Brown, Sam Cooke, Marvin Gaye, Aretha Franklin, Ike and Tina Turner, Solomon Burke, and others.

Dolphin was known for promising big paydays for artists, studio musicians, and songwriters, which did not sit well with some who felt they

Doo-Wop Redux

Across the country, shortly after the death of John Dolphin, Slim's Times Square Records in New York went into the reissue business by licensing vocal group 45s and pressing them on the Times Square Record imprint.

"Slim Rose was great at finding these obscure records, licensing the masters, and offering them at reasonable prices," said Nadine DuBois, author of *The History of Times Square Records*. "He had a vision even though he knew nothing at all about music."

THE "CLOCK" THAT TICKED, TOCKED, AND ROCKED

Beyond Elvis Presley, the only other artist to have a No. 1 rock 'n' roll hit prior to 1958 was Bill Haley and the Comets. "Rock Around the Clock" received one of the more carefully planned campaigns of the era.

Milt Gabler, who had founded the Commodore record store in New York a decade and a half earlier, was working for Decca Records in 1954 when Haley and Jimmy Myers struck a deal. Haley would make four singles a year, Decca would send out 2,000 promotional copies to radio disc jockeys, and full-page ads would be placed in the two top trade publications, *Billboard* and *Cashbox*.

Gabler convinced Haley to incorporate more of an R&B sound in his country music when they recorded Max Freedman's "Rock Around the Clock," which was cut first by Philadelphia novelty quartet Sonny Dae and the Knights, and released regionally in 1954. Sales of the Comets' version hit 75,000 copies soon after its release.

The record became a bona fide smash, however, in the spring of 1955 when it was used in the opening credits of MGM's *The Blackboard Jungle*. Re-released, it hit No. 1 and became an international hit, selling an estimated 25 million copies.

Cashbox named the Comets the best small instrumental group of 1955 and "Rock Around the Clock" the best record; the jazz magazine *Downbeat* tagged Haley as the top personality in R&B; and *Record Whirl* magazine named the band its favorite instrumental combo, Haley as favorite R&B artist, and "Rock Around the Clock" as favorite record.

Unlike Presley, Haley would never again hit No. 1.

Located on Broadway just north of 42nd Street, the shop could only hold about 10 people at a time but in 1959 it created a revival for the vocal groups and doo-wop acts of the early and mid-1950s. Some of the records he would press were only out of print for three to five years. It was a central spot for collectors to gather, and some dealers, such as Broadway Al Trommers, who has been cited as the first key oldies collector, would sell records outside the shop.

"Times Square Records was the first place and then you had Broadway Al and Bleecker Bob's, the Record Museum, House of Oldies, Relic Records— all places to find collectible records," said Lenny

Kaye, who created a sub-genre of rock when he curated the album *Nuggets: Original Artyfacts of the First Psychedelic Era, 1965-68* for Elektra Records.

Times Square Records moved to a larger space in 1963, but DuBois said most of his regulars found it too clean and sterile. "The old place had every surface covered in records and boxes and paper." The store was finally sold in March 1965 for $5,000.

Half a Century of Blues and Jazz in Chicago

Bob Koester started selling records in 1950 out of his dorm room at St. Louis University. He spent several years after college in St. Louis selling records before moving to Chicago and opening the Jazz Record Mart in 1959. In travel guides, it is often listed as the best jazz store in America and even after moving five times in the city of Chicago, it has continued to stay true to its roots in jazz and blues.

Aware of department stores and a few other specialty shops, Koester said, "it took me years to realize that I was doing something different. I didn't read *Billboard.* I didn't talk to a lot of other owners but I had long talks with Ross Russell," the Los Angeles record storeowner who created the Dial label to record Charlie Parker.

What Koester created in Chicago was a breeding ground for blues and avant-garde jazz, a hangout for the white blues fans such as Michael Bloomfield,

Bob Koester, shown in 2007, opened his first Jazz Record Mart in Chicago in 1959.

Paul Butterfield, and Charlie Musselwhite, who would introduce the genre to rock fans around the world. They were attracted to the store as much for the records as for the people who would visit, many of them artists on Koester's Delmark label— Buddy Guy, Junior Wells, Big Joe Williams, Magic Sam, to name a few.

Bloomfield and Musselwhite would eventually work at the Mart, as did a number of people who started their own blues labels. Bruce Iglauer founded Alligator Records, Michael Frank launched Earwig Music, Chuck Nessa did the Nessa label, and Amy van Singel and Jim O'Neal not only owned a label, Rooster Blues, they created *Living Blues* magazine.

A NEW MARKET FOR RECORDS

With the major labels controlling the distribution channels, entrepreneurial upstarts needed to come up with ideas that made financial sense for the buyers and were logistically plausible.

Tops was a Los Angeles-based label with a business model that put records where they had never been sold: the grocery store.

Two New Yorkers, watch repairman Carl Doshay and garment cutter Sam Dickerman, moved to Los Angeles in 1947 and started selling used records to markets, drugstores, and Five & Dimes. Doshay and Dickerman paid jukebox operators 5 to 10 cents for their used records and then resold them for 29 cents, less than half the price of a new record. The records were "guaranteed," meaning retailers did not have to pay for records they did not sell and could return them. Tops is believed to be the first label/distributor to use that system, which would become widespread in the 1950s.

Tops Music Enterprises wound up selling millions of records, locking in clients such as Woolworth's, Thrifty Drugs, and Sprouse Reitz.

In the 1950s they created a label, Tops, which hired sound-alikes to record hits of the day. The 78s would feature hit songs on both sides and would be sold for the bargain price of 39 cents or 49 cents. The majors sold their 78s for 79 cents.

Tops eventually sold off the distribution business and concentrated on making their knock-offs, creating extended-play 78s and then expanding into 45s and LPs. Business was so good that their manufacturing plant was operating 24 hours a day.

But as the label attempted to keep up with formats and musical trends, not to mention trying an ill-advised "tribute to big bands" series when the music was considerably out of date, it eventually was sold to a non-musical company. Tops went bankrupt in 1960.

"Delmark was premature in the blues market," Koester said. "There wasn't much reason to do it other than I thought it ought to be recorded. *Hoodoo Man Blues* (Junior Wells) was the first time a working black blues band went into a studio and recorded an LP."

Hoodoo did well in its time and Koester would market the store by printing the album cover on the front of T-shirts and a sentence on the back saying "I got it at the Jazz Record Mart." When *Hoodoo Man Blues* was issued on CD, it sold 6,000 copies quickly and has averaged about 4,000 a year. "Junior's other records," Koester said, "don't have that kind of success."

The blues, though, did not do anything for Koester's love of jazz. As a label head and salesman, he wanted to be in the business of the traditional jazz of New Orleans that dated back to the turn of the century. The store was opened to support his label, Delmark, which he had also created in St. Louis in the early 1950s. Originally named Delmar after one of the main drags in St. Louis, another business complained and he added the first letter of his last name.

He recorded local traditional jazz bands in St. Louis but found the market for that music to be quite slim. "In St. Louis," he said, "I found white people bought West Coat jazz and black people bought bebop."

Undaunted, when he moved to Chicago, he mentioned with pride, "it was the only store with traditional jazz and big band—basically a collectors store. Up until I bought major inventory, I bet I had only 125 to 150 new LPs because people were still collecting 78s. We sold a lot of Art Blakey and Miles Davis."

For many, 1959 represents the apex of modern jazz. Miles Davis's *Kind of Blue* and Dave Brubeck's *Time Out*, which featured "Take Five," were not only landmark albums artistically, they were bona fide commercial hits. That year also saw the first Atlantic Records release by John Coltrane, a few albums by Charles Mingus, and the first Bill Evans Trio record. In most stores, it is highly likely that

SPEED DEMONS

The 1940s saw one of the most aggressive ramping up of format changes, even though records were not even made for more than a year toward the end of the decade. The '40s opened with the 78 being embraced and closed with the unveiling of the 33⅓ long-playing album (by Columbia) and the 45 rpm single (by RCA Victor). It was not until 33⅓ and 45 rpms were introduced that the industry agreed on how to play records.

Early releases from RCA Victor played best at a variety of speeds between 72 and 81 rpm. A record compendium from 1916 advised that RCA titles be played at 76 rpm. And Emil Berliner, Edison's technological competitor in the 1880s, stated that his releases were made for 70 rpm.

When the 33⅓ and 45 formats were agreed upon, research was hastily shut down on another speed that was being looked at: 16⅔.

the top-selling jazz title was released in 1959. But not at the Jazz Record Mart.

That honor goes to Sun Ra and *Sun Song*. Originally released by Ra and his Arkestra as *Jazz by Sun Ra*, it was one of two titles that Koester issued on Delmark. The store's second biggest seller was a Charles Mingus and Charlie Parker album, *Live at Massey Hall*, which listed Parker as Charlie Chan due to contractual issues.

Prior to recording Wells, Koester had stuck with folk-blues musicians such as Big Joe Williams, Sleepy John Estes, and Speckled Red; on the jazz side, it was the pianist Art Hodes, the Dixie Stompers, and others.

"With a New Orleans jazz band, I would say I can sell 500 and the band can sell 500 if they're active," Koester said of his early days. "Selling 700 copies was pretty good. Speckled Red did 300 and that was a disappointment."

Speaking like a man who did his own inventory at the label and the store, he refers to albums by their catalog numbers—the Williams releases are 602 and 604, for example—Koester never kept track of how many Delmark Records he sold at the store.

Hoodoo Man Blues was released in 1965, "when white guys and Harvard types and people from New York City" were shopping in the store, Koester said. At the same time, Elektra was releasing the debut album from the Paul Butterfield Blues Band.

Having covered the sound of a Southside club on a Saturday night with *Hoodoo Man*, Koester ventured out to expose Westside blues to the world.

"Magic Sam was ahead of the white blues crowd," Koester said of the guitarist whose *West Side Soul* was released on Delmark in 1967. "I felt I was taking a chance by recording him." *West Side Soul* sold 1,700 copies that first year, which made

TOP 10 IN TIMES SQUARE

Times Square Records would issue monthly charts of the top sellers among the store's singles. While the rest of the U.S. was swooning to Elvis Presley singing "Are You Lonesome Tonight?" in January 1961, Times Square buyers were loading up on:

The 5 Discs: "I Remember"

The Edsels: "Lama Rama Ding Dong"

The Admirations: "The Bells of Rosa Rita"

The Elchords: "Peppermint Stick"

The Capris: "There's a Moon Out Tonight"

The Hi-Fives: "Dorothy"

The Channels: "I Really Love You"

The Channels: "Flames in My Heart"

The Continentals: "Picture of Love"

The Students: "Every Day of the Week"

Koester rethink his plans for the label. He had a deal with Riverside in place to reissue blues 78s issued on the legendary Paramount label. "But blues and avant-garde jazz felt more important."

The Association for the Advancement of Creative Musicians was headquartered in Chicago, making it a hotbed for heavily improvised jazz. Koester signed the pianist Muhal Richard Abrams,

Anthony Braxton, and two members of the Art Ensemble of Chicago—Roscoe Mitchell and Joseph Jarman. Jarman's *Song For* sold 300 copies, Abrams's *Levels and Degrees of Light* moved 200, and Braxton's debut sold 400. Braxton's landmark two-LP set *For Alto* sold 1,000 copies. For Roscoe Mitchell's *Sound*, 500 were pressed in stereo—which had no problem selling—and 500 were in mono. "Those crashed. I had to price them at 99 cents in the store. I wasn't a fan of that music," Koester said, noting that he has come to enjoy it more recently. "I felt it was too important not to release. It was similar to Ross recording Charlie Parker. We had some records go two years without shipping and some of the records sold so poorly, I had to drop their options."

Koester has never cared for pop music, and Bob Dylan is just about the only artist who does not fit the jazz or blues categories whose records and CDs have been stocked over the years—Dylan made it onto the shelves because his debut album featured songs that had been recorded by the old folk blues musicians.

Legend has it—and Koester does not remember this incident—he inadvertently provided a band name for James Osterberg and his friends. Osterberg, better known as Iggy Pop, was tossed out of the store and yelled at for unruly behavior. Koester referred to Iggy and his pals as "stooges."

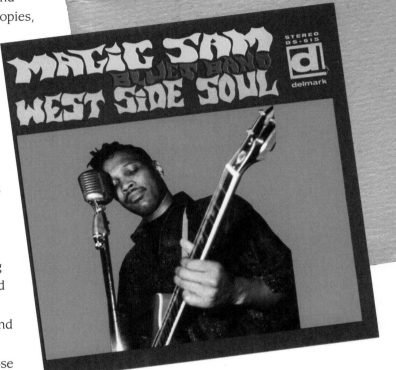

Guitarist and singer Magic Sam Maghett was one of the leading lights of West Side Chicago blues.

CHAPTER 4

TWIST AND SHOUT

NEON SIGNS WITH the words "hi-fi" and "stereo" hung in record store windows to attract listeners as the 1950s came to a close. Mono and 78s were largely viewed as things of the past, and the concept of high fidelity had become a crucial marketing ploy: RCA even released an orchestral album titled *Magoo in Hi-Fi*, a suite inspired by the poor-sighted cartoon character, Mr. Magoo. That kept the adults occupied, who were plunking down four or five bucks at a time for LPs by the Kingston Trio, Frank Sinatra, and the Broadway cast of *The Sound of Music* to play on their living room hi-fi consoles.

Launching the 1960s, the Beatles arrive as Tower Records begins its ascent

Meanwhile, the kids had the teen idols—Frankie Avalon's "Venus," Paul Anka's "Lonely Boy" and "Put Your Head on My Shoulder," and the goofy "Kookie, Kookie, Lend Me Your Comb" by Edd Byrnes. Bobby Darin's "Mack the Knife," the top hit of 1959, attracted teens and adults alike.

In retrospect it would become known as the greatest year ever for jazz as '59 saw the release of several landmark albums, among them Miles Davis' *Kind of Blue,* John Coltrane's *Giant Steps,* Charles Mingus' *Mingus Ah Um* and Dave Brubeck's *Time Out,* which featured the hit "Take Five." Nothing, however, was gripping the music world as a whole.

Step into a record store and you'd be likely to see the Top 40 singles in a rack by the front counter and a record player spinning the top hits, one at a time. LPs, and not necessarily a wide selection of them, might be stocked behind the counter, or you might bring an empty record jacket to the clerk, who would give you the LP upon purchase. In the bins, LPs were not divided by letter or artist, they were filed by style: male vocalists, female vocalists, black male vocalists, black female vocalists, classical, soundtracks, and so on. The LP explosion was just beginning to take off.

Elvis was in the Army, Buddy Holly had been killed, and the music industry began telling consumers what the insiders believe was the most noteworthy music of the day. The Grammy Awards were first handed out May 4, 1959 to recognize the music of 1958. They honored a TV soundtrack (Henry Mancini's *The Music from Peter Gunn*), a song performed in Italian ("Volare" by Domenico Mougno) and shut out Frank Sinatra, who had received 12 nominations. The hitmakers of 1958, among them Elvis Presley, Danny & the Juniors, the Platters, and the Coasters were ignored. The Grammys would continue to ignore rock 'n' roll until the Beatles were handed two trophies for their 1964 releases—best new artist and best performance by a vocal group.

The music industry—or at least the major labels—was not ready to embrace a rock 'n' roll world. Obviously, the Beatles changed all of that.

Rock 'n' roll was fad and trend-oriented. Lenny Kaye, creator of the mid-'60s *Nuggets* compilation, and David Budge, who would sing in a band called the Druids of Stonehenge before moving on to a series of industry jobs, were attracted to the doo-wop sounds of their New York neighborhoods.

"Rockabilly was exotic," Kaye said. "Group harmony was what I heard on the streets in Brooklyn and that was what I was drawn to. I continue to have a deep love for doo-wop."

And after shopping for years at an uptown store on Lexington that hipped him to the latest James Brown and other R&B records, Budge saw the Beatles "as four guys ruining music." But once they hit, they permeated. Ask adults born in the early 1950s and odds are the first single or album that entered their lives was by the Beatles. Even if it

Capitol Records heavily promoted albums by the Beatles in U.S. record stores at the close of 1964.

meant tangling with a record store clerk trying to push older styles on younger listeners.

"First time I went into a store by myself I asked for the Beatles 'I Want to Hold Your Hand.' You had to gear yourself up for that," said musician Peter Case, who led the Nerves and the Plimsouls before embarking on a solo career. "The guy behind the counter says, 'whaddaya want that for? Don't you want Percy Faith or "Victory at Sea"?'"

The Beatles made record buying habitual. Howard Wuelfing skipped out of high school at lunchtime to buy *The White Album* the day it was released, and timed the train ride back into New

Jersey so that he would make it back before the next period.

"When the Beatles came out, the word was out that it [a record] would go on sale at a particular time" at a store outside Nashville, said Del Bryant, whose parents Felice and Boudleaux wrote "Bye, Bye Love," "Wake Up Little Susie," and other country and early rock 'n' roll hits. "And you stood in line to buy *Meet the Beatles*. And *The Beatles' Second Album*. And *Rubber Soul*. There was nothing more fun than standing there talking about what you were going to buy with people. You were in sync with your culture."

Henry Diltz, who would gain fame as a photographer in the late '60s shooting album covers for Crosby, Stills & Nash, the Eagles, the Doors, and James Taylor, played banjo in the Modern Folk Quartet, which evolved from a straightforward folk unit in 1960 to a folk-rock band with electric instruments working with producer Phil Spector in 1966.

"When the Kingston Trio released records, you ran to the store, bought the album and ran home to listen to it," Diltz said. "You would keep putting the needle back to hear that lick or get that groove. That didn't happen again until the Beatles

> "In a way, it comes down to holy relics. If you are buying a record, you are buying a piece of the artist. If people treat it that way, there will be records and there will be record stores."
>
> —ROBYN HITCHCOCK, MUSICIAN

came out. You wanted to be first among your friends to have the album.

"Those covers were exciting. You couldn't turn on the TV and see these bands so the photographs were your connection with the band. That was as exciting as the music. When they released *Rubber Soul*, that picture was something else."

It was not enough to check in with the local department store or record shop and inquire about a hit. There was a desire for information.

"There were no release dates," said Bob Merlis. "And if there were, it didn't mean the store would have the record. You had to go in every day and ask 'is that new Mothers of Invention record out yet?'."

Adding to the confusion was the fact that the U.S. and UK were not in sync when it came to release dates, which Lewin's Record Paradise on Hollywood Boulevard capitalized on.

"It was the place to get bootlegs and imports," said Harold Bronson, one of the founders of the Rhino Records label. "Their reputation was based in the mid-'60s when they were the only known record store in L.A. to carry English rock imports. As the U.S./UK releases by major artists conformed in the late '60s, the store's appeal lessened."

Hale Milgrim was 13 when he convinced his father to add two bins of 45s and three bins of LPs to the family's Palm Springs, California, Toy Time store in 1960. First with his parents and then on his own with friends, Milgrim would make the two-hour trek to Los Angeles to go on record-buying pilgrimages. He, too, became infatuated with British imports, shopping initially at Lewin's Record Paradise in Hollywood and then the Groove Factory.

One discovery among the imports was the Jimi Hendrix Experience.

"Right after the Beatles, the one that really got my heart was Jimi Hendrix and I went and saw [him] as many times as I possibly could. One day I'm driving along and I hear on the radio that Jimi Hendrix is going to do an in-store signing at the Groove Factory, one of the few he ever did in his life,"

Milgrim said of the September 1968 event. Hendrix was headlining the Hollywood Bowl that night.

"It was a zoo. They took the doors off the hinges and put in curtains that were images of Jimi Hendrix's mouth so when you walked into the store, you walked into his body."

Are There Any More Stars?

By 1965, Glenn Wallichs, overseeing Capitol Records while his brother Clyde was running the Wallichs Music City store, estimated that 53 percent of all records were sold to teenagers. At Capitol he hired producers who were college age but the sales staff was still full of men from an earlier generation who saw the records by the Beatles and the Beach Boys as an easy sell.

Capitol turned 25 in 1967 and Wallichs was blunt about their position. "We're still looking for another great new artist," he said at the time. "We're still screaming about prices, competition, costs, and a hundred other problems. We are still struggling for our next big hit."

Wallichs milked its connection with Capitol and radio station KFWB, which had a studio inside the Wallichs' San Fernando Valley location and was just a few doors down from the Hollywood store. Among the promotional items created were the Beach Boys' "Spirit of America" backed with "Boogie Woodie" packaged in a sleeve that read "I

Was There KFWB Day! Wallichs Music City South Bay Store Opening Nov. 16, 1963." A June 1964 release was "Music City KFWBeatles" featuring one side of the Beatles talking and "You Can't Do That" on the flip.

Financing the Fads

The hits of the early 1960s were almost always tied in with a fad of some sort—the biggest was the British Invasion. On the singles side, there were a slew of dance records—"The Twist," "The Loco-Motion," "The Monster Mash"—girl groups, teen idols, the Motown sound, and folk-rock.

Peter Holsapple of the dB's got his first job at Reznick's, a record store in a Winston-Salem, North Carolina, shopping center.

"We sold a lot of beach music," Holsapple said of the music popular in the Carolinas in the '60s. "And of course, whatever was on the WTOB Pop Rhythm & Rock 'tunedex' that came on tiny sheets every week.

"The singles were plentiful at Reznick's. The main stock was in a browser, and the last copies were kept in greenstock sleeves with the sale record and reordering history marked on them. I found out eventually that Mr. Reznick didn't seem to

> "They were a library and a breeding ground for me when I was growing up—that's where I got all my influences and how I learned to play."
>
> —BOOKER T.
> FOR RECORD STORE DAY

return too many of his non-selling titles, and lots of weird vintage 45s were beneath the bins."

Until the Beatles, the Rolling Stones, and the Supremes took command of album sales in 1966, the decade was defined by soundtracks from films (*West Side Story, Mary Poppins*) and Broadway (*Camelot, Hello, Dolly!*), veteran singers (Louis Armstrong, Judy Garland), comedy (Bob Newhart, Allan Sherman, Vaughn Meader), and oddities such as Enoch Light's *Stereo 35mm*, the Singing Nun, and Frank Fontaine's *Songs I Sing on the Jackie Gleason Show*.

One store, however, wanted to make it clear it was different: Wenzels Music Town in Downey, California.

"They sold band instruments and had rehearsal rooms," said Dave Alvin, a Downey native who formed the Blasters there. "You'd be in there buying records and you'd see local bands practice. I saw the Carpenters in there before they had signed to A&M. Richard was doing a jazzy thing."

It would become the epicenter of surf instrumentals. Bill Wenzel and his son, Jack, opened Wenzels Music Town in Downey in late 1958. One half was a store for hi-fis and records, the other half was a recording studio. They created the Downey label and specialized in instrumentals, starting with a group called the Pastel Six. Their first hit would come from the Rumblers, "Boss!", but it would be the Chantays' "Pipeline" that put them on the map.

The Birth of Tower

Up north in Sacramento, Russ Solomon threw in the towel on his venture into record wholesaling. It was 1960 and the first two homes of Tower Records were open.

"I was broke," Solomon said, "so I concentrated on the retail store. Restructured and opened on the other side of town.

"The record business was staid. I came from general retail drug. Dad was in the chain business, places like Thrifty Drug. The idea of discounting and having loss leaders was very normal to me. It was not normal to the record business. They always thought themselves precious. It was a little ridiculous that to be competitive, this was a brand new idea."

Solomon took a page from Sam Goody's book and gave customers a reason to return to his stores. He focused on 45s, "and if you spent six bucks, we gave you a player."

He decided that Tower would concentrate on pop music and offer a large selection. "By attracting each of the micro-markets—country, R&B, classical, and on and on—it would work. I always thought of Tower as a bunch of stores in one building. Each constituency was a business of its own and that's what made it successful."

By the end of the decade, he had a store in San Francisco and would be eyeing property in Los Angeles on his way to building the most respected chain in the industry.

Tower had a unique approach. Previously, retailers had decided to either offer a vast

Russ Solomon, shown in 2004, opened Tower Records to offer a large selection and discounted prices.

The first Tower Records in Sacramento, California, photographed in its first year of operation, 1960.

inventory (Wallichs Music City, Sam Goody's) or discounted pricing (E.J. Korvettes).

The "preciousness" within the industry of which Solomon spoke was typified in an anecdote from Lee Cohen, who got his start in a Chicago record store and then moved to Los Angeles to work for Licorice Pizza. Discount Records, owned by CBS Records, was the largest chain in America and Cohen worked at the store across the street from the Chicago Lyric Opera. It was the city's largest record store. Opera stars such as Luciano Pavarotti would shop there, as did Studs Terkel and Pete Seeger.

"The store was set up so that it had every classical record ever made. It was all run by Big Dave. People would come in and ask 'Do you have Andre Previn doing Elgar?' We'd ask Dave and he would shout 'Angel 30975.' We'd get up on a ladder and get the album. Next person wants Stravinsky on Deutsche Grammaphon—he shouted the number. He knew exactly where they were.

"Big Dave was also an opera singer. He'd bring his music stand and if it was quiet or empty he would sing along with the opera records."

Outrageous: Hippie Music Takes Hold

For a new breed of record buyer, anything that was not rock 'n' roll was considered squaresville.

Record stores changed and had to offer what

was being played on FM radio or written about in *Rolling Stone*. Toward the end of the mid-1960s, WGLD, WLS-FM, and Leonard Chess' WSDM were tastemakers in Chicago and having an effect in the suburbs.

Paul's Recorded Music in Wilmette, Illinois, was run by people who appeared a bit square. "Yet he had all the cool 'underground' records," said Cary Baker, longtime music publicist. "I would tie up my bike, grab some albums, and often spent from 3:30 till dinner time in the listening booths. Though as far as I was concerned, I was on another planet."

Paul's carried albums by the Mothers of Invention, plus Kim Fowley's *Outrageous*, Robert Johnson's *King of the Delta Blues Singers*, Washboard Sam's *Blues Classics* on Arhoolie, and, of course, the blues greats who recorded for Chicago's Chess Records.

In Jersey City, New Jersey, Wuelfing was ready to visit a store besides the one he had been walking to for years. "The rumor was that there was an underground record store but I had to take a half-hour bus ride to get there. I find the place, and records are stacked to the ceiling—I remember having a sensory overload. I had no idea what any of the records were but I figured I had come all this way and I had to walk away with something. I saw this record, *Absolutely Free* (by Frank Zappa and the Mothers of Invention). Yea, I'm not gonna find this anywhere else. My cousin and I learned every line of that record."

The counterculture had moved in: Wells Street in Chicago, the East Village in New York, and Brady Street in Milwaukee, to name a few neighborhoods, had populations that resembled Haight-Ashbury in San Francisco.

"Discount Records didn't have the music you were looking for," said Keith Covart, who opened

GOING SHOPPING WITH JOHN DOE

"We knew that specialty record stores were out there," remembers John Doe of X and the Knitters. "I had been in one near Druid Hill Park on the west side of Baltimore in the early sixties, begging my mother to buy me Jackie Wilson's 'Lonely Teardrops,' which she didn't cave to my bawling and purchase. I think they also sold sodas and snacks, which is why we were there in the first place. But most records we bought were from the department and Five & Dime stores. The first 45 single I bought was 'For Your Love' b/w 'Got To Hurry' by the Yardbirds. I believe it was at Hecht's Department Store in the Mondawmin Mall. This was a couple miles down the street, across the tracks (literally) and bike-riding distance from home.

"The sad, unfortunate fact of riding double on a bicycle with a 45 single is that when you crash, the record usually breaks. At least this was the case with my first 45. Fortunately it was a split that could be popped back together so that the record played with only the slightest click as the crack went by.

"But as our teenage record-buying progressed through the '60s, most Rolling Stones, Beatles, Four Tops, Temptations, Supremes, Otis Redding, Doors, Hendrix, Janis Joplin, Spirit, Dr. John, the Band etc. records were bought at Hecht's or Hutzler's in either the Westview or Mondawmin Malls. Certainly nothing fancy or even well-stocked but it carried enough variety to feed our tastes from the mainstream, which at the time was rather broad."

Musician John Doe at Amoeba Music in Hollywood, 2009

Electric Fetus in 1968 with a partner who had been living in California and returned with new musical tastes. "There was no five-year, no business plan. Things just sort of happened."

Covart had been a claims adjuster and felt more comfortable in a record store than in an insurance office. The store's first location abutted the University of Minnesota, where people were rallying against the construction of buildings that were seen as dehumanizing. The store became a headquarters for community organizers and Covart even participated in a rent strike.

"Half of what we did was community," he said. "It was about people coming in and talking, hanging out."

One evening, either Keith or his partner forgot to lock the door at night. When they returned the next morning, "there were people crashed on the floor and notes on the desk. Ten or twelve dollars was left on the counter. Nothing was stolen. The vibe back then was wonderful."

These Boots Are Made for Selling

In 1969, the hottest Bob Dylan record was not released by his label, Columbia, nor sanctioned

"I found a record that changed my life at White's in Peekskill, New York. I only wish I had bought it then—my life would have changed that much sooner. Instead, no matter how many times I looked at the original Elektra release of *Nuggets*, I just couldn't pull the trigger. I guess my double album budget was reserved for more important records like *Wheels of Fire*."

—IRA KAPLAN, YO LA TENGO

CITY SHOPPING IN THE '60S

Keith McCarthy, a music industry veteran, speechwriter, and publicist, started buying records at a torrid pace in 1968 and has never eased up. Most of his buying has been in New York City and these were among the best shops around, according to him.

Downstairs Records, 1475 Broadway at 42nd Street.

"More familiarly known as Times Square Records, it was down a small flight of stairs at the northeast corner entrance of the 42nd Street Broadway subway. The store was shaped like a small shotgun apartment, with a low ceiling and boxes and boxes of records—albums and singles, chart toppers, and promos smothering both sides. I remember poring over boxes of promo 45s from indie labels including Cameo-Parkway, Tico, and Jubilee, five for a dollar! It was also one of the few places you could find Latin music below West 125th Street."

Sam Goody's, 49th Street off 8th Avenue.

"Sam Goody's was it in New York if you were a music fan. The guys who worked there had written books and contributed to music magazines, and some achieved notoriety, like Jeff Atterton, a Brit early-jazz enthusiast who hated everything newer than the big bands. One day, one of his colleagues, Freddy, 'schools' me and takes the new Sonny Rollins album, *East Broadway Rundown*, puts it on the stereo, and plays it at 45 rpm. It sounds exactly like Charlie Parker. 'You dig where Sonny's coming from?' was all he had to say. Sam Goody's was the first (and only) major record store I can remember having cutouts and remainders, priced from 69 cents to 99 cents, in a separate store directly across the street from the flagship store."

8th Street Record Store, 8th Street between McDougal Street & Fifth Avenue.

"A cutout store, maybe the best ever, chock full of every genre of music, major and independent labels alike, beginning at 99 cents an album up to maybe $2.99. Original Atlantic, Savoy, and CBS albums were cutouts—it's where I learned to take a chance and buy an album if I recognized the producers or session musicians or arrangers. On a Saturday afternoon, you could drop $60 and walk out with more records than you could carry."

The Record Hunter, 42nd–43rd Street and 5th Avenue.

"Primarily classical, it carried music by Harry Partch, old opera titles, and lots of everything else in between. A retired New York distribution exec said to me that, in the 1970s and '80s, on a per-square-foot basis, Record Hunter did more business than any record store in the world."

by the artist himself. The album was *Great White Wonder*, a two-LP set consisting of nine songs recorded with the Band in Woodstock, New York, twelve songs recorded in a Minneapolis hotel room, four tracks of talking, and "Living the Blues," recorded directly from a television set when Dylan appeared on *The Johnny Cash Show*.

It was the first hit bootleg. The place to get it, *Rolling Stone* reported, was in Los Angeles where the records were sold openly and printed in nearby Gardena. Five radio stations—KCBS in Santa Barbara, KNAC in Long Beach, KRLA in Pasadena, and KMET-FM and KPPC-FM in Los Angeles—played the album. A private investigator was hired to calculate its availability; he found the LP in 23 of the 45 stores he visited.

"It takes a while to learn," musician Dave Alvin said, "but there's usually a box under the counter. That's how I got *The Million Dollar Quartet*," a popular bootleg of a jam session featuring Elvis Presley, Jerry Lee Lewis, Johnny Cash, and Carl Perkins years before it was ultimately released commercially.

The first time *Rolling Stone* reported on the Dylan record, in September 1969, there were 2,300 copies sold. That number would crawl to 40,000 within a year as, it was widely believed, other bootleggers would make copies of the album and distribute it in other parts of the country.

"I just thought they were different kinds of records," said Richard Foos, who sold LPs at swap meets and a Santa Monica electronics store before opening Rhino Records in 1973.

Prices for the album varied wildly. The wholesale price was $4.50 each and most places sold it for $6.50 and up. One store, the Psychedeilic Supermarket in Hollywood, had it for $12.50. Berkeley's Leopold's, the first student co-op record store in the country that priced records 50 cents above cost, sold their first batch for $6.67 and a second shipment for $5.24. They sold 3,000 copies.

The popularity of the Dylan boot paved the way for a Rolling Stones concert album recorded in Los Angeles and Oakland in 1969. *Liver Than You'll Ever Be*, billed as a recording by the Greatest Group on Earth, was hailed by *Rolling Stone* magazine as "one of the finest albums of 1969."

Leopold's sold 1,600 copies in two weeks. A Chicago store sold 2,000 copies for $5.50 each. By contrast, Music 5 in San Francisco had Procol Harum's *Whiter Shade of Pale* and the Mamas & the Papas *Farewell to the First Golden Era* on sale for $3.74.

Columbia Records threatened to sue anyone associated with bootlegs; the company's mounting fear concerned the illegal release of recordings of Dylan's Isle of Wight festival performance.

Until a new law was enacted in 1971, national statutes had been lax and states differed on the illegality of bootlegs. Tennessee, for example, enacted a tough law, but Alabama had no problem with illicit work at pressing plants.

Music Millennium in Portland, Oregon, shown in 1969, was among the new breed of stores pushing new artists.

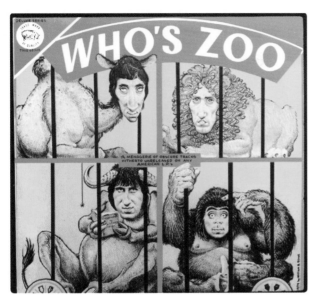

The first bootlegs were of live recordings but eventually boots would feature collections of songs not released in the U.S. such as *Who's Zoo*, which included UK recordings and a side devoted to performances from TV shows.

The popularity of bootlegs spurred labels to issue live albums such as Crosby, Stills, Nash & Young's *Four Way Street* and Elton John's *11-17-70*. Dylan's *Self Portrait* was rushed out after it was noticed tapes had been stolen from Columbia's vaults.

Eventually, the owners of two small stores in Los Angeles, Norty's and Do-Re-Mi, were charged with selling bootlegs. In late 1971, Ode Records sued Emmanuel Aron of Aron's Records for selling a Carole King bootleg and asked for $1.5 million. Warner Bros. and Atlantic sued seven companies

for a total of $1 million over boots of Neil Young, Jimi Hendrix, Van Morrison, Led Zeppelin, CSNY, and Jethro Tull. All the cases were settled out of court.

"It was a cat and mouse game at a couple of stores," said Gary Stewart, a clerk at Rhino Records in the 1970s when bootlegs still made their way into independent record stores. "We'd put them in the used section."

Gary Stewart, a clerk at the Rhino Records store, shown at one of the store's famous parking lot sales. He would become an A&R executive at the label.

MY FIRST RECORD

Cameron Crowe, filmmaker and journalist.

"Cream's 'Sunshine of Your Love' b/w 'SWLABR.' It was kind of like buying a *Playboy*, walking back into the house where rock was still banned. It was 69 cents. Came home with it in a brown paper bag. My sister was in on it. That whole experience was lodged big time in my brain and it made me want to write about it."

Robyn Hitchcock, musician (Soft Boys, Egyptians, solo artist).

"My first record was 'It's All Over Now' by the Rolling Stones. The big guys who worked there had what Americans call pompadours. I was a wee pre-pubescent boy being confronted by these larger boys who had obviously been through the change. I just remember being so self-conscious. Will they laugh at me? Will they beat me up? I played that record only twice because it reminded me so much of the embarrassment."

Peter Buck, musician (R.E.M.).

"When I was five and six I was obsessed with radio and playing my parents' records. For my sixth birthday, my dad gave me a $20 record player and my parents said I could pick out two records. I got 'A Hard Day's Night' and a Disney thing, 'The Ballad of Swamp Fox.' I would play those endlessly, one after the other. One day my dad said, 'Let's go buy you a couple more records.' I think I realized I had driven him completely batty. I still have that copy of 'Hard Day's Night.'"

Susanna Hoffs, musician (the Bangles and solo artist).

"Carole King's *Tapestry* and James Taylor's *Sweet Baby James* and very soon after that Neil Young's *After the Gold Rush*. I was very aware of the interconnections, how they sang and played on each other's records. Joni Mitchell was in there, too."

Ryan Adams, musician (Whiskeytown, solo artist).

"Sonic Youth's *Sister*, bought at Record Bar in the mall in Jacksonville, North Carolina, and Black Sabbath's *Born Again*, bought by my grandmother at Rose Brothers Furniture, which sold pretty much everything but groceries."

Lenny Kaye, musician (Patti Smith Group), writer, creator of *Nuggets*.

"For Christmas my dad bought me a record player in the shape of a conga drum. We went to Vogel's and I got 'It's Only Make Believe' by Conway Twitty, 'The Purple People Eater' by

Ryan Adams, 2009

Sheb Wooley, 'It's All in the Game' by Tommy Edwards, and 'To Know Him is to Love Him' by Cathy Carr, which was the version I thought I had heard on the radio. I really wanted the Teddy Bears'. First album was *The Everly Brothers' Greatest Hits*."

Lucinda Williams, musician/songwriter.

"I was 11 years old and wasn't shopping in record stores yet. The Beatles had arrived the year before, in 1963, so the first record I owned was probably *Meet the Beatles*."

Peter Jesperson, label head (Twin/Tone, New West).

"*Meet the Beatles*. In January 1964 at Record Land in Hopkins, Minnesota."

Butch Walker, musician/producer.

"*The Monkees Greatest Hits*. 5.99—The Nice Price was what it said on the sticker. That and Kiss' *Destroyer*."

Matthew Caws, musician (Nada Surf).

"*Goin' Back to Indiana* by the Jackson 5. I found it in the lone rack on the electronics and entertainment floor at Gimbel's on 86th Street and Lexington Avenue in New York, five blocks from where I grew up. The cover art was amazing, comic-book-style lightning and explosions framing a photo of the brothers onstage in fringed half-pop-star/half-super-hero outfits. My favorite track was 'The Day Basketball Was Saved,' a seven-minute skit narrated by Bill Cosby. I must have been about nine."

Steve Wynn, musician (Dream Syndicate, solo artist).

"*Willie and the Poor Boys* (by Creedence Clearwater Revival). Bought it at the May Co. at Wilshire and Fairfax (in Los Angeles). I had been given records, but I'm not sure that I had ever bought a single before."

MY FIRST RECORD

Peter Holsapple, musician (the dB's, Continental Drifters, Holsapple-Stamey).

"My first record was a Decca 45 of Bert Kaempfert & His Orchestra's 'Afrikaan Beat,' which was the theme song to the Sandy Becker kids' TV show in the New York area. That was followed by the yellow Atco single of 'Alley Cat' by Bent Fabric and His Orchestra. The first album I bought with my own money was *Bare Wires* by John Mayall and the Bluesbreakers. For many years, I could decline the family tree of Mayall with the confidence of a Latin student with a simple verb."

Ben Vaughan, musician.

"On my eighth birthday, my mom took me to Woolworth's in Camden, New Jersey, and told me I could buy one record. I picked 'Twist & Shout' by the Beatles on the Tollie label. It was not an easy choice as there were at least four Beatles records on sale on four different labels. I remember being confused because none of them looked alike. I was already a prime target for branding, I guess."

Daniel Glass, president and owner, Glassnote Records.

"The first time I got a promo was Hot Tuna's first album. That was a big deal to a kid."

Paul Epstein, owner, Twist & Shout, Denver.

"'The Chipmunks Meet Dr. Dolittle.' It connected TV, movies, cartoons, comics, and music. First album was *A Hard Day's Night*. I still have my copy."

CC Adcock, musician.

"I was 6. I went into some chain in a mall in Baton Rouge (the only mall in Louisiana at the time—'77) and was immediately taken by the cover art of a Kiss record. Anyway, my mom couldn't get behind it so I left with Captain & Tennile's 'Love Will Keep Us Together,' which I'll still break out at an all-night, living room dance party. Great track really."

Jim White, musician.

"'The Ballad of the Green Berets' by Sgt. Barry Sadler when I was 10 years old."

Linda Pitmon, musician (drummer).

"I had received singles as gifts and I stole one, J. Geils Band's 'Love Stinks.' I wanted to learn the drum part. They caught me. It was at a Target (in Minnesota) and they called my parents and they came to get me. But they forgot to take the record from me so I slipped it behind my back and walked out. I spent the rest of the week practicing the drum part."

Matt Kivel, musician (Princeton).

"BoyzIIMen 2. A classic. My parents gave us two 45s when we got a Fischer-Price player. One was Bert and Ernie's 'Rubber Duckie.' The A-side was in English and the B-side was in Spanish. The other one was Madonna's 'Papa Don't Preach.'"

Harold Bronson, co-founder of the label Rhino Records.

"'The Battle of New Orleans' by Johnny Horton because I liked American history. Interesting that in an unconscious way my love for history directly relates to the historical aspect of reissuing. Another early single purchase was 'Itsy Bitsy Teenie Weenie Yellow Polka Dot Bikini' by Brian Hyland, which reflected my love of novelty records. The first album was *My Son the Folk Singer* by Allan Sherman. My family was at another's for dinner, and the two brothers played the album for me."

Doug Herzog, president, MTV Networks.

"I took the money from my bar mitzvah and went to Sam Goody's in New York and bought *Sly & the Family Stone Greatest Hits*, Three Dog Night's *Golden Biscuits*, and Honey Comb's *Want Ads*. It was 1972."

John Brenes, owner, Music Coop, Ashland, Oregon.

"The Coasters' first album. I still own it. My cousin came down to L.A., this was in 1958, and we went to Wallichs Music City and took it in the listening booth. I had maybe 75 45s but this was my first LP."

Chris Vanderloo, co-owner, Other Music, New York.

"Growing up in Delaware, my parents would always have us mowing the neighbors' lawns or shoveling snow in the winter. One year I had made about 15 bucks by lunchtime and I asked my mom if I could walk to the record store. I bought Neil Young's *Live Rust*."

Manny Maris, co-owner, Downtown Music Gallery, New York.

"*In the Court of the Crimson King* by King Crimson. I was 12. Up until then I had only been exposed to classical music and I didn't care for pop music. That changed my life. I was willing to buy any record with the word 'king' on it."

Bob Merlis, author, publicist, former Warner Bros. executive.

"Frankie Ford's 'Sea Cruise' was my first 45. Bought at HyGrade Electronics on Church Avenue in Brooklyn."

OVER UNDER SIDEWAYS DOWN

THERE WAS LITTLE reason to spend much more than $3.25 for an album as the 1960s came to a close and the 1970s ushered in a whole new cast of characters to the record store universe. The difference became the environment. One store had a friendly staff, another had considerable back catalog, yet another had shelves packed with apparatus for smoking pot, black-light posters, and alternative magazines. Record companies began to provide advertising to the stores in the guise of posters, stand-ups, and other point-of-purchase displays that may have brightened up—or cheapened—your local store.

Hippies and misfits adapt stores to reflect the tastes of Woodstock Nation and the kids of the '70s

As the years passed, record labels increased the number of promotional items created for stores.

Record shops began putting up bulletin boards filled with notices about concerts, bands seeking members, and people looking for rides to gatherings that were both political and musical in nature.

These were the early models of "lifestyle stores" that would emerge decades later, places where like-minded people gathered. Rather than commerce, the unifying factor was the music, which was no longer heard in listening booths— you heard whatever the guy behind the counter decided to play. Odds were that it was fresh and exciting.

Radio had its hits and record stores had theirs, usually albums that needed to be heard in their entirety like side two of the Beatles' *Abbey Road*, side four of Jimi Hendrix's *Electric Ladyland,* the debuts from Blind Faith and Crosby, Stills & Nash, and the guitar solos of Santana's first two albums. Record stores became crucial in creating the soundtracks of people's lives.

A year is not what pops into Jim Greenwood's mind when he's asked when he decided to open his first Licorice Pizza record store in Long Beach, California. It was the albums that were selling: "The first Creedence Clearwater Revival, first Led Zeppelin. I remember The Rolling Stones' *Beggar's Banquet.*"

It was 1969, half a year before the Woodstock Music and Arts Festival in New York would come to define a generation that was rejecting the values of their parents. Not entirely a hippie, but Greenwood knew he was not heading into corporate America.

"I got a degree in finance from USC and I knew I did not want to go into that business. My father was in retail and in some small way I understood retail."

Greenwood was fortunate that his father owned a building that could house the first Licorice Pizza. His rent in that first store, opened two years prior to Tower coming to Los Angeles, was $200 a month.

The interior of Village Music, in Mill Valley, California

The final years of the 1960s were a landmark for a new breed of record retailers eager to make music specialty stores the hippest places in town. Rock festivals were galvanizing crowds of like-minded music fans, proving that a substantial audience was forming with music at its core. The musical spectrum was being blown wide open: LPs were no longer just hits collections or items for adult listeners.

The local "music shop" was undergoing a transformation. All-encompassing shops that emphasized the creation of music—places where records were sold alongside guitars, metronomes, and sheet music—would quickly give way to stores where recorded music was the focus. In plenty of cases, particularly in college towns, the concept of the head shop was being flipped around: Records in the front; water pipes, rolling papers, and black light posters pushed to the side cases.

"The first thing I did was get rid of everything but the records," said John Goddard. He started working at Village Music in Mill Valley, California, when he was 13 and took over the store just after college in 1968. "There were three bins of rock, 20 bins of easy listening, 40 bins of classical.

"I had the goal of stocking the entire Folkways

A love for records inspired the rare pairing of Jerry Garcia and Elvis Costello at an anniversary party for Village Music in April, 1989.

catalog," which at the time had 1,300 albums. "I wanted to make sure I had something for any taste. When Jerry Garcia came by (in 1969), he could buy Joseph Spence and Django Reinhardt, he didn't have to go to a folk record store and then a jazz store."

Goddard, whose shop had a storied run up through the end of September 2007, was a prime example of the new breed of shopkeeper. He knew his music, knew popular tastes, and had a vision for what his store would be. It was a story that would be repeated around the country in locally owned record shops that catered to rock audiences, which sprang up everywhere. In Goddard's case, it helped that Mill Valley was 14 miles up the road from the hippest city in America. San Francisco had partially recovered from 1967's Summer of Love, when 100,000 young people invaded the Haight-Ashbury district to become part of the growing counterculture rooted in the city.

Ed Stasium, leader of the band Brandywine prior to his vaunted career producing and engineering records by the Ramones, Talking Heads, Gladys Knight and the Pips and others, saw firsthand the sudden differentiation between the instrument stores and the record shops. He regularly shopped for records and instruments at Gregory's Music in Plainfield, New Jersey.

"I remember going into Gregory's the day after I saw the 'New' Yardbirds at the Village Theater in New York City in November 1968. It was my first rock show. Jimmy Page used a wah-wah, I had never seen or heard anything like it in my life. I asked the counter person at Gregory's if they had such a device and the dude looked at me like I was nuts. He had *no* clue."

While the world was being thrilled by *Sgt. Pepper's Lonely Hearts Club Band* (released in June 1967), the major labels were looking to bring in a new wave of artists, many of whom would reshape the majors—Jimi Hendrix at Reprise; Janis Joplin, Laura Nyro, and Electric Flag at Columbia; the Band and Quicksilver Messenger Service at Capitol.

The energy of youth made commercial opportunities abundant. *Rolling Stone* magazine hit newsstands for the first time on November 1, 1967 with John Lennon on the cover. And Tower Records, with its two homes in Sacramento, found a closed grocery store in late 1967 to become its base in San Francisco. It opened in early 1968.

By far the San Francisco location was Tower's largest outlet and it would become ground zero for many of owner Russ Solomon's experiments. They stacked boxes upon boxes of records near the entrance, they hung enormous promotional artwork on the outside walls, and they attracted a clientele of stars that would include Joplin, members of the Grateful Dead, and Carlos Santana. Outrageous stunts—bringing in a live elephant painted pink to celebrate The Band's *Music From Big Pink*—were commonplace.

"We were at Columbus and Bay and all the record labels are two blocks away," Solomon said. "The store was a runaway hit from day one."

Since so many record executives were shopping at the store, "they were aware of how (album cover art) on the promotional wall was part of the tie-in with radio and retail. You could do a promo and a record would take off."

That scene was being played out across America. In Austin, Texas, the first hip place was Inner Sanctum. "That was when Austin exploded with live music," said Bill Bentley, an author, record producer, and publicist who moved to the Texas capital from Houston in 1970. "Every in-store would have a keg and free beer. It was the first store that didn't feel like it was owned by The Man."

As a teenager in Hamburg, New York, outside

Buffalo, singer-songwriter Peter Case found refuge at Cox Records, owned by a chain-smoking woman about 30 or 35 years old who was dating Freddie Green, the guitarist in Count Basie's band.

"She liked me because I liked jazz," Case said, recalling that it was the first place he heard Jimmy Reed, John Handy, Pink Floyd, Taj Mahal, and Muddy Waters. "It was her store so she would play anything we wanted, especially weird records. One day this record came in by Jimi Hendrix and we didn't know who he was. She put it on and it turned the world upside down."

A riot erupted in the streets of Isla Vista, California in February 1970 while Hale Milgrim was managing the local Discount Records. The National Guard was sent into town as protestors burned down a Bank of America building.

Hale Milgrim, who would go on to hold high-ranking positions at several record labels, got his start at Discount Records in Berkeley, California.

"Any street you walked down in Isla Vista was blaring music," he said. "And when the National Guard came into the record store, we put on The Rolling Stones' 'Street Fighting Man.' They said 'you are not only going to turn off this music, you are going to close this store and get the hell out of here right now.'"

Aquarius Records, which is touted as the oldest independent record store in San Francisco, opened its doors in 1970. Denver had Underground Records, which Paul Epstein, owner of Denver's Twist & Shout, started visiting in 1968.

"We had just moved from New York and we find this great, totally '60s head shop with cool imports," Epstein recalled. "I knew I could live in Denver then." He was eight years old at the time.

"Everything we were selling was $2.99. It didn't matter if it was Elton John's brand new *Tumbleweed Connection* or the Beatles or the Stones. And people came up to the counter with stacks of records. Retail did everything it could to keep the volume up."

—HALE MILGRIM, DISCOUNT RECORDS MANAGER, BERKELEY

Singer-songwriter Nicolette Larson shopping at Discount Records in Berkeley in 1975

Record Riot On Sunset Strip

San Francisco's role as the epicenter would be short-lived as chains and labels saw Los Angeles as the key place to do retail, with the Sunset Strip as ground zero. Tower Records was the first with a location on the Strip; Licorice Pizza moved in kitty-corner from the Whisky a Go Go.

The Atlanta chain Peaches opened on Hollywood Boulevard and Wallichs Music City continued to do brisk business at Sunset and Vine. And all the new players were staying open until midnight.

"It was not out of the ordinary for the store to do $1 million in business on a Saturday," said Cary Mansfield, who managed the flagship Wallichs Music City in Hollywood from 1974 to 1976.

Solomon saw L.A. establishing itself as "the fountainhead" of the music business and he contacted a friend from Liberty Records to scope out a location for him. A space was found on Sunset; it had been a restaurant and, coincidentally, was occupied by Earl Muntz, who invented the 4-track tape cartridge, which lost out as a format of choice to the 8-track pioneered by William Lear of Lear Jets fame.

"It was pure Hollywood," Solomon recalled. "Everything in the front of the store was flashy and it was all junk in the back. (Muntz) had gone broke building these tape machines. We wound up tearing down the building and building a new one, which we were able to do for practically nothing."

Cary Mansfield was the manager of Wallichs Music City, West Covina, in 1973. He later went on to manage the flagship Hollywood store.

Adam and the Ants took over Sunset Boulevard for a promotion at Tower Records in 1980.

Despite all the clutter on the retail scene, each store carved out a niche. Licorice Pizza's Greenwood did research on what goes into a decision about where to shop and it boiled down to service, price, or convenience. "So we went for service and convenience. In some instances price, too." But Greenwood knew that would be insufficient. "We were truly thinking about satisfying the senses," he said.

To that end, free licorice would be handed out to customers or kept by the front counter. Incense was burned in the stores; couches were added to give people a place to sit and listen to music. Boxes of records were placed on the floor and displays unique to each store covered the walls and ceiling. The senses were pounded in those stores.

"One thing was driven into me and I passed that along—we were a friendly, customer-service-

OPPOSING VIEWPOINTS

Rock bands of the late '60s and early '70s connected with their audiences in one specific area: fashion. By performing and being photographed in their street clothes rather than outfits designed for the stage, performers forged a bond with their fans. And there were two ways to look at it. Bob Merlis, co-author of *Heart & Soul*, a book on R&B from 1950 through 1978, said: "I remember being in Sam Goody's and making a decision for myself about whether I should buy a record I had not heard. I see the first Mother Earth album and I concluded that, based on their appearance, I wanted to meet them. I bought the record figuring there's a 50 percent chance this is pretty good. And 40 years later, I was still working with (Mother Earth lead singer) Tracy Nelson."

The novelty wore off for singer-songwriter Robyn Hitchcock by 1972. "Just because something had a gatefold and a picture of some hairy people on it playing seven-minute long songs didn't mean it was any good. I shuddered when Led Zeppelin and Uriah Heep came out, heavy music based on riffs and hi-fi equipment. I listened to the tune rather than the EQ of the bass and the thunder of the drums."

oriented store. Everything was geared toward being friendly. There was no competition with Tower—they had every record that was out there. Music Plus was a little cheaper, but they didn't have the selection. And The Wherehouse had more locations.

"The record companies responded to us. If they wanted more attention, like bigger displays, they'd come to us. But there was some integrity—some things they asked us to do that we refused."

Licorice Pizza and the other Southern California chains grew quickly. Each time a Licorice Pizza got its financial footing, Greenwood would open another. Each one would be larger than the last, going from the original 800 square foot store to 1,200 square feet until the stores reached 8,000 square feet.

The company, named for a routine by the folk duo Bud & Travis in which they comment on alternative uses of poorly selling vinyl, had several groundbreaking moments. Licorice Pizza was the rare record store that advertised on TV—"we have the tastiest music in town" was the focus. They "guaranteed" every record they sold. Customers were allowed to return any record for any reason and get store credit. In '74, they offered a dollar off to anyone who would streak a store. They'd stay open for 24 hours and have all-night sales.

"We'd get a limo and go around to all the stores and we'd see lines," Greenwood remembered. "All through the night—for a dollar off."

Unlike the other competition, Tower Records handled its expansion slowly. It did not open a second L.A. store until 1975, locating it within the Westwood Village that abuts the University of California at Los Angeles. At that time, Tower began an advertising campaign as "the largest record store in the known world."

But Solomon is convinced to this day that Tower's instant rise in visibility owed to a tragedy in which it had no role: the death of Janis Joplin. The singer died in a hotel not far from Tower Sunset on Oct. 4, 1970. It made national news.

"It was a story for a few days," Solomon said. "The national and international news channels would film in the store. We got coverage on the six o'clock news and all of a sudden we were a hit. People came from England and Japan, there was a huge upsurge. When *Pearl* came out it started selling like mad." Prior to Joplin's passing, Solomon had only seen one other death cause a significant ripple in sales—and that was when he was selling records out of his father's drug store. The singer was Al Jolson.

The advent of new stores coincided with new musical styles and a new approach to album artwork.

"The first Crosby, Stills & Nash album is the granddaddy," said Henry Diltz, the photographer who shot the famed cover of the trio on the front porch of a house in L.A.'s Laurel Canyon.

"I was playing a radio station game to try to win records so that I would have an excuse as to how a record got into the house. I won *Buffalo Springfield Again*."

—CAMERON CROWE ON GROWING UP IN A HOUSE WHERE ROCK MUSIC WAS BANNED

Diltz and art director Gary Burdon were hired by the band rather than the art department of the record label. They created covers that received the approval of the artists and their management, then handed them over to the labels. At the time, Diltz noted, certain elements always needed to be on covers—the label's logo, a designation of either stereo or mono, the band's name, and the catalog number. Burdon shook up convention by placing a small Atlantic logo above the mailbox to the left of Graham Nash.

"You see the genius," Diltz said. "Then he says 'I want it to be printed on the back side of the paper.' Everything else was printed on the glossy side and

Henry Diltz shot photos for the bands, not the record companies, breaking ground on new styles of record covers and the materials they were printed on. Shown here are photos for the debut album of Crosby, Stills & Nash, The Doors' *Morrison Hotel*, and James Taylor's *Sweet Baby James*.

he wanted to use the textured side. The record company went nuts. But (the managers) David Geffen and Elliot Roberts had insisted on artistic control." For their second album, *Déjà vu,* Crosby, Stills, Nash & Young were able to have the cover done in the style of a hymnal.

Crosby, Stills & Nash became a springboard. Diltz was hired to shoot The Doors' next album, which was unnamed at the time. They, too, wanted to use the grainy cardboard for the album that would become *Morrison Hotel,* which was named for the skid row flophouse in which Diltz shot it. Years later, Morrison Hotel would become the name of Diltz's gallery.

Diltz had been a musician in the Modern Folk Quartet in the early 1960s. "We didn't have any say in our record covers. The label would hand us the artwork and say 'here's your cover.'" After becoming a photographer—he shot publicity stills for Buffalo Springfield, the Monkees and the Lovin' Spoonful—he made his mark shooting pictures of musician friends, which gave his album covers a different look and mood. For certain artists, album covers were no longer the creations of art departments, which had not always respected the photographs.

The use of Diltz's work on James Taylor's *Sweet Baby James* and *Hums of The Lovin' Spoonful* irked him because of the graininess.

"That was my way to get the feeling of the record—make it an automatic thing when you look at the guys. I had a simple approach—it wasn't a photo session, it was gathering of friends. Gary [Burdon] was an extremely friendly guy and very cool, everybody liked him. I was already their friend."

Some of the bands that trusted Diltz—and the resulting covers—became legendary. The Eagles and Diltz left the Troubadour in L.A. one night at 2 a.m. and drove two hours to Joshua Tree in the desert to shoot their first album. Diltz and Burdon took America to Big Sur for one cover and to a Native American oasis near San Diego for another.

New World Disorder

At the end of 1971, when *Billboard* did its tally of the top artists for singles and albums, nine of the

> "In 1968, the name Electric Fetus made sense. You had the Electric Flag, Electric Ladyland."
>
> —KEITH COVART, OWNER, ELECTRIC FETUS IN MINNEAPOLIS

album artists and six of the singles artists had no baggage from the 1960s. It had very quickly become a post-Beatles world.

Warner Bros. Records took out an ad in the final edition of *Billboard* that year touting it as the best year in the record label's 13-year history. The Grateful Dead, Alice Cooper, Van Morrison, James Taylor, Gordon Lightfoot, Neil Young, T. Rex, Seals & Crofts, Black Sabbath, Jimi Hendrix, the Faces, and the Beach Boys were cited for having hits for the label that year.

The explosion of suburban malls meant several types of record stores were going into cities and towns across the country. Columbia Records sold its chain, Discount Records. National chains were taking up space in indoor malls and regional chains were finding homes in strip malls. The mom & pops were scattered, usually wherever they could find cheap space to rent. Naturally, kids wanted the stores they worked in to be as hip as possible.

Gene Rumsey, who in 2003 became general manager of Concord Records—the label that orchestrated Ray Charles's comeback, worked in a mall outside Philadelphia in the early 1970s. We Three was one of three record stores in the Plymouth Meeting Mall, Al Franklin and Sam Goody's were the others.

We Three's specialty was oldies, but the key was "being staffed by knowledgeable guys and having a relationship with the customer. The clerks wore ties and greeted every customer. It's the sort of thing you don't find today." He left the store floor in 1976 to become a buyer for the chain.

John Kunz, who would partner with Waterloo Records founder Louis Karp in Austin, was working at a mall store, Disc Records, when he and a manager convinced the corporate chiefs that Austin could stand to be a bit hipper. From that idea sprang Zebra Records in 1975.

Stores made up their own rules, some of them silly, some of them designed to increase business. If a record went on the in-store sound system at the Hollywood Peaches and everyone working hated the music, the record would be removed and thrown across the room until it broke.

Displays were not always ordered from higher-ups either. "We created a massive display for Patti Smith's *Horses* at the front of the store because

Fitting in with the Pacific Northwest's ecological bent in the 1970s, this windmill was erected on the roof of Music Millennium in Portland, Oregon, to power the store's turntable.

we liked the record. But it had to be something we thought would bring people in and something we thought (the label) would pay for," said Henry Deas, night manager of the Hollywood Peaches from 1972 to 1976.

On the Jersey shore between 1969 and 1974, a single, small store provided one of rock music's top historians with an astounding education. "The Dealer helped define my taste more than any other institution or entity," said Bob Santelli, executive director of the Grammy Museum, who previously ran the Experience Music Project in Seattle and the educational department at the Rock and Roll Hall of Fame and Museum in Cleveland. "The owner moved to San Francisco and it closed, creating a huge void that has not been filled."

Santelli was initially a customer of The Dealer and became an employee while also playing rhythm guitar and singing in bands. In fact, most of the store's employees were in bands, some of them members of the Asbury Jukes and a short-lived horn-based band that Bruce Springsteen led.

"The owner was a typical *paisan* from North Jersey, but he had tremendous knowledge. If he said it was good, you bought it. It was so one-on-one. You went up to the desk and he would talk to you about your tastes and then turn you on to an album you didn't know existed. The Sons of Champlin became hugely popular because he told people 'you need to understand—this is a good band.'

"Half the state's fans of the Allman Brothers were made because he loved that first album. It spread like that. We became disciples of Jo Jo Gunne and the first Doobie Brothers record, the black and white album that nobody else bought. It was the first place we heard reggae. You could talk music, argue about music—it was the embodiment of the store/hangout," Santelli reflected.

School Kids Is In

Eric Brown was in Athens, Georgia, when he came up with an idea that would bridge all those worlds. The store name was School Kids. It would be a cooperative and anyone could own one, but the franchisee had to locate each store in a college town. It did not matter if the store name was one word or two, or even misspelled.

Blair Tanner owned Chapter III Records in Gainesville, Florida, named after an album by Manfred Mann. He sold that store to become part of the School Kids empire and open shops in Bloomington, Indiana, and Knoxville, Tennessee, homes of two major state universities.

Steve Bergman, a student at the University of Florida and a Chapter III employee, decided to drop out of college and become part of Tanner's team after helping to set up School Kids stores in Tuscaloosa (Alabama), Atlanta (Georgia), and Columbus (Ohio). Tanner set up and then sold the Knoxville store to become partners with Bergman in a Schoolkids in Ann Arbor, Michigan.

With $500, a handshake deal, and a van full

LIBERACE IN HOLLYWOOD

After a concert in the early 1970s in Hollywood, Liberace ventured into Peaches Records on Hollywood Boulevard dressed in, what else, a sparkling, jeweled jacket. It was an odd celebrity sighting—the employees were more accustomed to rock bands like Tom Petty and the Heartbreakers. (Drummer Stan Lynch was an employee.)

"We had older people in the neighborhood so we always had his records on hand," said Henry Deas, the Peaches night manager from 1972 to '76.

Deas got Liberace to autograph three albums, one of which was promptly framed with a peach crate and hung. A day later, Deas was reprimanded. "My boss said it was a waste of inventory."

Jazz legend Dexter Gordon visited Schoolkids, Ann Arbor, in 1977. From left to right: Steve Bergman, founder/owner of the Ann Arbor store; Gordon; Michael Lang, buyer and manager; unidentified assistant manager; Al Bray, assistant manager.

of LPs, Tanner and Bergman drove to Wolverine country to open Schoolkids in a tiny space on the third floor of a downtown building. After constructing their own bins, they put out a single copy of every record they carried with the intention of replacing each as it was sold.

"My first order of business," Bergman said, "was to say we're going to write down everything we sell. The idea of writing down what we sold bothered Blair and he fought it. It sounded too anti-music to him."

Bergman picked a perfect time to open. Columbia Records had sold its Discount Records chain, and the sales people servicing Detroit had no customers. They needed to treat someone properly so it became Bergman, who received

in-store visits from Dexter Gordon and Iggy Pop within a few months of opening.

After just six months, Bergman's future father-in-law offered him two-thirds of the money needed to buy out Tanner. He raised the other third, went into business for himself, and became the first to drop out of the co-op. In one form or another, the store remained open for more than 30 years.

Rhino Infects Retail with Humor

The thriving music industry was squarely hitting the mainstream outlets. It left room for a separate universe in which to establish itself—alternative retail, which found its genesis in west Los Angeles. Surly and opinionated clerks, bizarre promotions,

Rhino Records in Los Angeles carved a niche as an alternative and eccentric record store.

a list of banned customers, and an inventory that emphasized the obscure defined Rhino Records, a store that truly moved to a different beat than all others.

"First time I went to Los Angeles," Waterloo's Kunz said, "I made a pilgrimage to Rhino Records. I remember being so impressed by the sign on the door. 'Sorry, we cannot hold the entire Miles Davis and John Coltrane collections until you get paid on Tuesday.'"

Gary Stewart, who worked as a clerk at the store and then in the A&R (Artists and Repertoire) department at the Rhino label, first learned about the shop when he was in high school, especially from people who ran other record stores.

"My annual treat to myself, after I saved money to buy lots of records, was to ride my bike to Tower," Stewart said. "I walked in there [Rhino] on a weekday before [the annual Tower trip] and they had a cutout bin that blew my mind. I bought the Yardbirds, Lovin' Spoonful, *Happy Jack* by the Who, Fats Domino *Legendary Masters*. Incredible prices. That was it. It was rock snob heaven and rock neophyte hell. And I was both."

As the collectibles marketplace has grown over the years, an increasing number of record store devotees find themselves wondering 'Why didn't I ask that clerk to give me that poster?' And there are plenty of record store managers from the '60s to the '90s kicking themselves for not holding onto the odd-shaped disks, colored vinyl, or picture discs.

"I shall always regret not buying U2's *War* picture disc at Wax Trax in Chicago," said Cathy Maestri, an avid collector of U2 and other Irish rock bands. "It was $18 and they had a ton, so I figured I could get one later. They're now running just under $100 on eBay."

Colored vinyl and picture discs have long been oddities. While certain albums are famous for being released in color—Elvis Presley's *Moody Blue* in blue, Grand Funk's *We're An American Band* in gold, David Bowie reading *Peter and the Wolf* in green, Jimi Hendrix *Live at Winterland* on clear vinyl, Dave Mason's *Alone Together* in marble—most of the releases are special editions. The Beatles' *White Album* on white vinyl and the *Thriller* picture disc were introduced as limited editions long after the albums were initially released.

There were 100,000 copies of *We're an American Band* pressed on gold, for example, but only 200 picture discs were pressed of Wings's *Back to the Egg*. That 1979 picture disc was strictly for Paul McCartney's friends, family, and co-workers and is widely considered the most valuable McCartney record among collectors.

The rarest of the rare, however, are items limited to a single country. Among them: the Japanese picture disc of Rush's *Fly By Night*; the U.S. 10-inch of "Xanadu" by Olivia Newton John and ELO that was abandoned in 1980 after only 31 copies were made; Madonna's UK picture disc of "Erotica" that was recalled after the art was deemed too risqué. The never-released U.S. picture disc of Michael Jackson's 1993 album *Dangerous* saw its value skyrocket after the singer's death in June 2009. At the

One of the first picture discs, released by Vogue Records in the mid 1940s

A limited-edition picture disc of Madonna's "Like a Prayer"

time, Madonna's "Like a Prayer" picture disc was fetching more than $40.

The first picture discs were released in May 1946. The Vogue label began issuing 78 rpm, 10-inch records with illustrations that corresponded to the song titles. The most common of the titles was "Sugar Blues" by Clyde McCoy and His Orchestra, one of the first Vogue releases. It is believed 74 different discs were released before production ceased in April 1947.

Limited edition colored vinyl and picture discs are still being released to this day.

Rhino has its origins in a side corner of an audio equipment store called Apollo Electronics in Santa Monica. Richard Foos, studying sociology in college, had the record rack concession at Apollo. After a few years of not making much money, he got the boot. His new retail operation consisted of buying used records and bootlegs, and then selling them at a swap meet in the South Bay south of Los Angeles.

"On Saturday, you'd go to Aron's," Foos said of the popular store in the mid-Wilshire district of L.A., "and there would be a line of people early in the morning to get the records." Aron's would sell the albums practically by the pound and a healthy stack could be purchased for $3. Foos, a jazz and blues aficionado, would then charge a buck apiece for each LP.

Harold Bronson, who would run the Rhino label

with Foos after working at the store, was a fellow collector. "Somebody told me about this guy who had the record concession because you could go there and get the bootlegs and cutouts cheaper."

In October 1973, Foos set up shop at 1716 Westwood Boulevard, sharing space with an electronics repairman who operated in the back. Eventually Foos sufficiently stocked the place to be able to take over the entire, rather small, space.

Aron's was Foos's model. And that was a store where he would spend more time than money. "I might have $2 so I'd get a $1 album and spend hours and hours figuring out which four 25-cent albums I'd buy." On weekends—for about three years—he continued to sell records at swap meets. Foos was not a fan of the music of the day, singer-songwriters, disco, soft rock, progressive rock. "I

so hated the music until '77 when punk came out." To top it off, Foos said, "being a clerk at a record store was boring for me."

Foos and Bronson created a label to manufacture and release 45s. The first single was "Go to Rhino Records" by Wild Man Fischer, an eccentric singer who recorded an album for Frank Zappa's Bizarre label in 1968.

Fischer, Foos said, was "the first recording artist I ever met. In Wallichs Music City, '68 or '69. Wild Man Fischer comes up and introduces himself and I'm so excited because my brother was always talking about him. He was going around the (Sunset) Strip saying 'do you want to hear a song for a dime?' I thought that was so cool."

As the Rhino store started to catch on, to bring more levity into it, Foos and Bronson invented weeks-long blocks of specialty days. Among the highlights were "C" student day, in which anyone who brought in a report card proving their grade point average was a below a "C" would get a free record. Days were dedicated to reggae, Peter Noone of Herman's Hermits, Millard Fillmore's birth, Paul Simon, and Flo & Eddie, who were scheduled to show but never did.

Only one promotion backfired—the Make a Record Contest. The winner, chosen at random, would have a chance to become a recording star; Rhino promised to release their song with a picture sleeve. This contest became a curious footnote in Rhino history.

Richard Foos (right) opened the Rhino Records store and created the label with Harold Bronson (left).

Rhino issued its first single in 1975.

"Turning people on to music was part of the job."

—JIM GREENWOOD, LICORICE PIZZA, L.A.

Aron's Records, shown at its original location in Los Angeles, was a huge draw for those looking to stock up on LPs.

> "I love the smell of them. I love that people actually care for and know about the music they are selling."
>
> —NEKO CASE
> FOR RECORD STORE DAY

Richard Foos (left), who co-created the Shout! Factory label, reunited with Harold Bronson in 2009.

"Chris Madden," Bronson said as if the contest were held last week. "She was kind of like Linda Ronstadt and I thought the song was pretty good. It was pressed, but she wouldn't let us release it. Releasing it basically meant putting it on the counter and pushing the box forward. It was Rhino. We had a picture sleeve with a drawing. It's actually the rarest Rhino release."

Despite a sensibility that seemed completely geared for the college-age crowd, Rhino rarely pulled in UCLA students.

"The store was never a success—too countercultural, a little too uncomfortable for moms to come in to shop for their kids," Bronson said. "Richard and his sense of humor permeated the store. I latched on to that—making the retail environment fun."

RECORD STORES IN FILM

Once record stores became signifiers of hip, they made their way into movies of the early 1970s. Robert De Niro's Travis Bickle bought a Kris Kristofferson album for Cybill Shepherd in *Taxi Driver*; Goldie Hawn won an Oscar for playing a Greenwich Village record store clerk in *Cactus Flower*.

When Alex and his lady friends go vinyl shopping in A *Clockwork Orange*, covers of some of the hippest albums of the day can be seen. Among them: Pink Floyd's *Atom Heart Mother*; Tim Buckley's *Lorca*; John Fahey's *The Transfiguration of Blind Joe Death*; Chicago's *Chicago Transit Authority*; and Neil Young's *After the Gold Rush*. Alex asks for the then-fictional band the Heaven Seventeen.

High Fidelity and *Empire Records* are the two best-known films to feature record store settings. Among the others are: *Velvet Goldmine*; *This Is Spinal Tap*; *Hannah and Her Sisters*; *Before Sunrise*; *Mo' Better Blues*; *Quadrophenia*; *Pretty in Pink*; *Chasing Amy*; *Peggy Sue Got Married*; *Next Friday*; *Knocked Up*; *(500) Days of Summer*.

And while it does not include a store, it does exquisitely capture the nature of record collecting and how it controls a person's soul: *Ghost World*.

Alex and his friends shopped for records in *A Clockwork Orange*.

CHAPTER 6

SINGLES GOING STEADY

STACKS OF BOXES of LPs greeted customers as they entered Tower Records. Peaches stores turned album covers into art by framing them with fruit-crate wood. The key, whether it was a mom & pop store or a small chain, was to cover every surface with an image and dazzle shoppers from the minute they walked in the door.

Most record stores were set up the same way: a check-out counter at the front door, a row of tapes behind the counter that forced a customer to ask for a specific title, and from two to five rows of albums with rock in the front, and classical and country in the back, adjacent to the discounted titles and cutout bins.

Disco and new wave rattle the chains one track at a time as the '70s wind down

The walls were telling. The images—mostly posters and album covers stapled to the wall with the occasional dangling artifact—were an indicator of the store's hip factor. Most of those posters were put there because the employees loved the music. Consider 1974. A store wall with items promoting Frank Zappa's *Apostrophe*, *David Live* by Bowie, King Crimson's *Starless and Bible Black*, and Weather Report's *Mysterious Traveler* would be the sort of place an adventurous rock fan would want to hang. That collection made it easy to forgive the store for promoting the Bay City Rollers as well.

The middle of the 1970s sparkled in record stores of all shapes and sizes. *Frampton Comes Alive*, *Saturday Night Fever*, *Rumours*, Stevie Wonder, Paul McCartney, Elton John—those records and artists kept the industry climbing, eventually becoming a $4 billion a year business. The singles marketplace from the mid- to late-1970s was one dance hit after another, the pop charts filled with mostly upbeat disco tracks and the occasional slickly produced R&B ballad designed for slow dancing.

"A hot record came out—Earth, Wind & Fire—it wouldn't make it into the warehouse," said Daniel Glass, owner of the label Glassnote Records, who worked as a DJ and at a wholesale outlet in New York in the late 1970s. "The mom & pops would line up with cash in their hands. We'd just rip open the boxes and sell them off the loading dock."

Chains across the U.S. were big on discounts, in-store signings, and displays designed in-house. Go to one location of a chain and the displays would be pushing Linda Ronstadt and the Eagles; drive across town and the walls would be covered with record sleeves and posters promoting Bob Dylan and Paul Simon.

There were perks galore, most commonly free promotional copies of albums for the employees and free concert tickets for the store managers. As Keith Covart, who opened Electric Fetus in Minneapolis in 1968 says, "I'm a bit deaf from too many front-row seats."

The transition was nearly complete from the old-style music shops that sold sheet music and instruments in addition to records. Wallichs Music City shut its doors at Hollywood and Vine in 1977. While it had eliminated listening booths, it carried musical instruments and sold records at list price until the bitter end.

"People actually thought Wallichs had better quality records because the price was higher," said Cary Mansfield, who managed the store from 1973 to '76. The labels stopped issuing the store any credit and cut off its supply of new disks. "They had bought so many pianos and organs—and that they had to pay for up front—but that stuff wasn't selling. Being put on hold and having Music Plus down the street discounting records is why it went downhill."

Besides, the upstarts were making music exciting. Peter Jesperson started working at Oar

David Byrne and members of Talking Heads met fans at Oar Folkjokeopus in Minneapolis after the release of their debut album in 1977.

Folkjokeopus in Minneapolis in 1973 and soon thereafter was managing the store.

"We were so excited about records, [the owner] stepped back and let me run it. It wasn't like other places. We sold everything. We were the bohemian neighborhood—we didn't have boundaries. It was whatever is good. There was a little bit of the *High Fidelity* snobbery—laugh at someone because they had never heard *Blonde on Blonde*."

The new chains in Los Angeles—Tower, Licorice Pizza, Music Plus, and The Wherehouse—put boxes of records on the floor, they filled the walls with promotional material strictly aimed at young music fans, and played music that was usually hip and always current over the in-store sound systems. At Oar Folkjokeopus, named for albums by Skip Spence and Roy Harper, "we wouldn't put up promotional posters for things we didn't like,"

Jesperson said. "A Columbia records rep comes by and says, 'We want to put these up in windows.' I tell him no because we don't like the record. He says, 'You'll never get a Columbia promo ever again.' Yea right."

Each store felt distinctive, and that owed to relationships.

"We were better friends with certain labels," noted Jim Greenwood, owner of the Southern California chain Licorice Pizza, singling out A&M. Licorice Pizza put healthy promotional pushes into several A&M acts, having the greatest success with Cat Stevens, Supertramp, and Joe Jackson.

"A&M Records would come to the office and play us records they were excited about," Greenwood said. When A&M reps brought Jackson's *Look Sharp* to them in early 1979, "they played three tracks for us and we went nuts."

As a promotion, Licorice Pizza "guaranteed" that their shoppers would love *Look Sharp*. They quickly sold 5,000 copies of the album. "I think we got 10 records back," noted Randy Gerston of Licorice Pizza.

Joe Jackson was one of the surprise hits of 1979, the first year that the music industry slumped after 25 straight years of growth. The year lacked the smashes of 1978—the *Saturday Night Fever* soundtrack, the Rolling Stones' *Some Girls*, and Billy Joel's *52nd Street*—but there was more to the story. A slow Christmas buying season in '78 led to massive returns of unsold albums;

labels were cutting back on staff and money spent on promotional activities; blank cassette tapes became a booming business; and the summer yielded few major hits. "Major" at that time meant artists capable of selling 3 million copies of an album with the potential of hitting 10 million—numbers that would be staggering in the 21st century.

As one record store pontificator pointed out, something that becomes huge—in this case disco—does not become small, it goes away. While, as a genre, the punk and new wave scenes of the 1970s did replace the sales of disco, they also assumed a significant place in the culture. Just as the underground stores of the 1960s provided a forecast for the early 1970s, toward the end of the decade, small independent stores were demonstrating the need for alternatives. The smarter chains picked up on it quickly.

Doug Herzog spent a summer working at a Peaches store in Rockville, Maryland in 1979. He recited what sold: "Donna Summer, the Knack, Blondie, Supertramp, Graham Parker, Nick Lowe and *Labour of Lust*. Lowell George dies and we all wore black armbands for a week."

This Is the Modern World

The punk records—singles, LPs, and imports— "were at the core of our store," recalled Gary Stewart of Rhino Records. Oddly enough, Rhino

Indie meets underground in 1977 with the opening of Recycled Records in San Francisco.

moved into temporary quarters from August 1977 to April 1978, a time Stewart refers to as "the flowering of punk."

"There was a big bright line between commercial rock and underground rock, between what you heard on the radio and what you had to seek out in small stores and mail-order catalogs, between Elvis Costello and Bruce Springsteen, even," said Eli Attie, whose writing career has taken him from music criticism to political speeches to scripts for television.

"There were only 43 punk singles so you could collect them all," said Robyn Hitchcock. "All the singles had picture sleeves. There was a fetish element."

Robyn Hitchcock checks out some vinyl after an in-store performance at Amoeba, Hollywood, in 2009.

Singles are featured prominently at Lawrence Record Shop in Nashville, Tennessee.

Bob Merlis, who produced two compilations of B-sides for Warner Bros. Records, *Attack of the Killer B's* and *Revenge of the Killer B's*, *reflects*, "Not enough can be said about indie picture sleeves on 45s. They defined the era. Things like Graham Parker on pink vinyl. Patti Smith and 'Piss Factory.' Blondie's 'X Offender' before they were on Private Stock. People who bought those things were the bellwether. You didn't have magazines writing about this stuff."

The 45, largely shunned by the rock buyers who had become strictly album-oriented by the end of the 1970s, became the format of choice for punks, many of whom were paying for their own recordings, creating their own labels, or signing up with independents that could not afford to pay a band for an entire album.

"The whole punk rock scene was predicated on independent singles," said R.E.M. guitarist Peter Buck, who decided what to buy based on reviews in fanzines. "It was a calling card. Nobody expected to see money off it, but maybe (by releasing one) we'll get more shows, get it into stores. You could sell them at shows, but we were never that gung-ho about selling them. Some shows you'd only sell one.

"It makes you look like a real band. You could take it to radio stations. You could have cassettes, but a single is something they would want to play."

It was a throwback to the 1950s when indies would record groups for singles only, and to the 1960s when acts would be signed to a singles deal before securing a contract to do an entire album. The Byrds, to use an example that paid off handsomely, signed their first deal with Columbia Records to record only a 45. Once "Mr. Tambourine Man" scaled the charts, they were brought on as album artists.

Harold Bronson would travel to London and bring back singles to sell at Rhino, starting with Nick Lowe's "Heart of the City" b/w "And So It

Goes." The store sold out of Devo's debut single three times. Rhino would also attempt to get people to buy imported reggae records.

"Until the early 80s, it was underground," said Gary Stewart who worked as a clerk at the Rhino store and later in A&R at the Rhino label. "It was as much a cult thing as punk."

R.E.M.'s Buck was visiting his parents in Southern California in 1981 about 50 miles east of Westwood, the section of Los Angeles where Rhino was located, just south of the UCLA campus. Rhino was, he said, "the sort of store you would read about in *Trouser Press* and other magazines." R.E.M., which started when Buck met Michael Stipe at Wuxtry, the record store in Athens, Georgia, where Buck worked, cut its first single for the Athens label Hib-Tone.

"I walked in and said 'Hi I'm in this band in Georgia and we get good reviews. We've got this record.' The two guys say 'we don't take consignment.' 'What if I give them to you and you don't have to give me any money unless you sell them?' The guys looked at each other

and said OK. I left four copies and I came back and they were gone but there was no money because there was no record of it."

Bleecker Bob's in New York was a landmark for punk records, especially singles. Henry Rollins considers his first visit to the shop one of the single greatest record store experiences in his life. Rollins, Ian MacKaye (Minor Threat, Fugazi, and co-founder of Dischord Records), and a few friends had driven to New York from Washington, D.C., to see Sham 69 play at Hurrah's.

"There was no way we weren't going to check out the legendary Bleecker Bob's. I had my list of

Punk progenitor Jonathan Richman in 1983 near the singles counter at Rhino Records

Peter Buck (shown in 2009) and Michael Stipe met at Wuxtry in Athens, Georgia.

wants written down and asked Bob if he had this one, that one, etc. The more I asked, the more angry he seemed to get, like I was offending him by asking him if he had these records, thus implying that he might somehow not have them. He almost threw the records at me as he pulled them out of boxes. What a haul. Among many records I got that day was the first Misfits single, three bucks. It was like that. Those days are over, of course, but experiences like that don't diminish with time."

Cary Baker had a similar experience at Bleecker Bob's while visiting New York from Chicago. "I asked him for 45s by Buzzcocks, the Clash, Stiff Little Fingers, and the Cramps. 'What's wrong with the Viletones?' Bob snarled, pushing his house label's 45-rpm release. 'Nothing's wrong with the Viletones. But I'll take Buzzcocks, the Clash, Stiff Little Fingers, and the Cramps.' He paused. And paused some more. 'What's wrong with the Viletones?'"

Eli Attie made the leap into punk-new wave singles with the purchase of a Canadian pressing of Elvis Costello's "I Don't Want To Go To Chelsea." The store clerk, Peter Holsapple, had recommended it to him.

"I took it home and instantly decided I'd made a huge mistake, that it was the worst song by the worst singer I'd ever heard in my life," said Attie, a writer on *House* and *The West Wing* TV shows. "But I played it again. And again. And again—about 12 times, before deciding that it was actually better and cooler and edgier than all the classic rock I'd been buying and hearing on the radio. After hearing that one song, I chose a side and a sensibility that have defined my taste in almost everything since then."

The singles department at Music Maze was run by George Scott, a bassist for the Contortions, James White and the Blacks, the Raybeats, and 8 Eyed Spy with Lydia Lunch. Holsapple remembers his taste running from amelodic no-wave rock to pure glossy pop like the Bay City Rollers. He died of a heroin overdose.

"Single City was this narrow counter in the back of the store where the 45s lived," Holsapple said. "For years after his [Scott's] death, we'd find

little rants on some of the (sleeves), warning that the record enclosed was a total piece of shit. He was smart enough to buy lots of copies of things like 'Stickball' and 'Shaving Cream' by Benny Bell. He also had a box of things like 'Little Johnny Jewel' by Television on ORK Records, or 'Piss Factory' by Patti Smith. He also showed me how easy it was to empty a record store at closing time simply by putting on 'Paralyzed' by the Legendary Stardust Cowboy or 'Agitated' by the Electric Eels. We'd watch 'em run for the door and laugh."

Naturally, those singles, imports, and LPs were not in every store. Greg Shaw, the late owner of Bomp!, the label that became a store, would give bands lists of the stores that were willing to carry their records.

Bleecker Bob's in New York's Greenwich Village had one of the best selections of punk singles in the 1970s and '80s.

POLICE AND THIEVES

"When people today call the unfortunate widespread practice of illegally downloading music *stealing*, I have to laugh," says Michael Shelley, recording artist and DJ. "Inside I'm thinking 'Stealing?! You call that stealing?' You see, in my day you had to take the bus to the New Rochelle Mall, shove records under your coat, and nonchalantly walk out of the store with the Nick Lowe and XTC import 45s. Now that was stealing!

"My short career as a kleptomaniac was brought to an end when, while visiting my divorced father in Los Angeles, I was caught at the Tower Records Sunset Strip location committing larceny. I thought I was safely on my way home when I was tapped on the shoulder by a giant security guard who simply said 'You know what you did.'

"Back in the office I remained cool, as the clerks joked around with me and let me look through the two-way window while we waited for

my father to bail me out. Luckily, they weren't going to press charges."

"On the walk home, my Dad asked 'Is this because you're angry about the divorce?' The honest answer would have been 'Divorce? What divorce? Oh yeah, you're getting a divorce. No, this has nothing to do with that, I just really needed those import seven inches!' But not wanting to look a gift horse in the mouth, I dutifully burst into tears and gave my father what he wanted—yes, it was all about the divorce. . . . "

Gary Calamar kept an eye out for shoplifters while managing Moby Disc in Santa Monica in the early 1990s.

First with the Nerves and then the Plimsouls, Peter Case made his way across the country: Val's Halla and Wax Trax in Chicago; Oar Folkjokeopus in Minneapolis; Hideo's Discodrome in Cleveland Heights, where members of Devo, Pere Ubu, and the Dead Boys hung out.

"The little record stores were the center of punk and power-pop—they were centers of knowledge," Case said. "In every town where it came together, we'd play a gig and hang out at a store. There was a whole network of super music fans. No one was getting rich."

The Hip Kids in Boston

Mark Kates ran the Beastie Boys' label Grand Royale before starting his own Fenway Records. He marvels at the musical retail landscape of the late '70s in Boston.

"It is hard to imagine these days, but in the late '70s, Harvard Square had to be the one of the best record store neighborhoods on the planet," he said. "Besides the Harvard Coop, there was the amazing NE Music City, Discount Records, and the used stores. Deja Vu in Harvard Square was my go-to for bootlegs and other values. Eventually Newbury Comics and Tower swallowed up the others."

Newbury Comics grew into the most powerful and popular chain in New England in the 1980s and '90s, eventually running 28 stores within a 100-mile radius of the Boston flagship: Hartford, Connecticut, to the south; Portland, Maine, to the north; Amherst, Massachusetts, to the west; Cape Cod to the east.

It started as a comics store in 1979 with a few pieces of music in the Back Bay section of Boston, when the area was mostly tenements. Mike Dreese dropped out of M.I.T. to open the business while his partner John Brusger finished his degree. Dreese would sell comics to prostitutes or just about anyone who would knock on the front door and wake him. He lived in the back of the store before moving into a series of rooming houses in the area.

"We did it with no debt," Dreese said. "It started with $2,000 and a comic book collection. My partner worked at a rug factory. I worked at a convenience store, worked the breakfast shift at McDonald's, and washed dishes at a hospital." They quickly realized that comics did not have the appeal of the music. And once a friend who worked as a wrestling promoter decided to give them his record collection to sell, "we went from 2 percent music to 75 percent.

"The energy of punk and new wave was completely unaddressed by mainstream retail," Dreese said. "It was a combination of faux punks, real punks, and the gay community, people who were not into Strawberries or Harvard Coop. There was a lot of angst.

"This thing broke in England and dozens and dozens and dozens of bands were flying to Boston and New York, doing a show and going back to the UK in 1979 and up through '81. In Boston there was a phenomenal scene for these acts, many of which were unsigned."

Dreese's father worked in NATO and often flew to London for meetings. Dreese tagged along, went to the hottest store in the city, Rough Trade, and created an importing company. Soon, Newbury Comics was responsible for 40 percent of Rough Trade's business in the U.S.

"These two brilliant guys from M.I.T not only built an unbelievably successful and world-renowned business, but also did so off the back of

JIM WHITE BUYS HIS FIRST ALBUM

Singer-songwriter Jim White, whose debut album was titled *Wrong-Eyed Jesus,* was living in Amsterdam, Holland, and scheduled to fly to New York to visit a good friend who had sold his record store, became a top male model, and quit that to work as a lobster fisherman. "He loved music, more so than anyone I'd ever met. I wanted to present him with some exotic musical gift, something he couldn't get in the states, so I wandered into a random Dutch record store.

"I'd never read about music, never sang anything but hymns, never paid any attention to breaking artists or Top 40 nonsense or anything like that so this cluttered Dutch record store was as foreign a place as any I had ever been. I walked up and down the aisles utterly bewildered by the selection of sexually ambiguous New Romantic bands like Spandau Ballet, Dead Or Alive, and Orchestral Manoeuvres in the Dark.

"I was beginning to despair when an album cover caught my eye. It featured two midgets and a scruffy-looking man wearing suspenders. Although I'd never heard of the guy, I bought the album just on the basis of the cover. It just looked right. A few days later in New York I proudly presented the album to my music-phile friend and was

delighted that he was stumped by the artist and album title.

"When he dropped the needle on the record, as the first guttural howls came leaping out of the speakers, he winced conspicuously. My friend said, 'Where the hell did you get this crap?' Chagrined, I said, 'Um . . . Holland.' 'God,' he moaned, 'this guy sounds like a freaking wino.' And I agreed—the guy did sound like a wino. So I told him, 'Yeah, I meant to get you another album. I'll exchange it and get you that new Dan Fogleberg album.' He seemed placated as he handed me the repellent album back.

"I tucked it in my suitcase, took it back to Holland, bought a record player, and on that record player that wino's album stayed until the grooves were worn off. I listened to it four, five, sometimes upwards of 10 times a day every day. Slowly but surely I felt empowered by the wino's words, felt the chains of irrational religion falling away as I became a transformed creature. Taking cues from the album, I began scouring the streets of Amsterdam for evidence of beauty in unlikely places, and found treasures wherever I looked. The treasure had been there all along, I just needed some twisted genius to point it out to me."

The album? Tom Waits' *Swordfishtrombones*. Coda: "Joe Henry produced my third album. We'd hired Ralph Carney to play sax on a song and so Joe called Tom Waits, who played with Ralph for years, to ask how to best utilize Ralph's immense but erratic talent. Tom gave Joe some pointers, then asked who the artist was. When Joe mentioned my name, Tom Waits said, 'Oh yeah, the Jesus guy.' Tom Waits thinks of me as the Jesus Guy. My work is done here."

Jim White at Amoeba Music, 2008

the most exciting musical era of my life, post punk," Kates said. "Along the way they also had a record label and a magazine lest anyone doubt their cultural commitment."

Newbury Comics quickly expanded its outreach, operating as a concert promoter, fanzine publisher, and record label, Modern Method, which issued 26 records during its lifetime, among them the *WBCN Wicked Good Time* and the *This is Boston, Not L.A.* compilations. Aimee Mann's first recording, "Brains and Eggs," was a Modern Method release as was November Group. In 1980, the first issue of *Boston Rock* magazine was published.

"We had control of the mouthpiece. *The (Boston)*

Globe wasn't covering the scene. The (alternative weeklies) *Phoenix* and *The Real Paper* did a little. I was shipping it to 500 mom & pop stores. Our press run wasn't huge—7,000 to 8,000 with 3,500 of those paid for. We wrote about bands coming to town—Billy Idol, Robert Fripp, Gang of Four— and that connected us to the musicians and the musicians to the store.

"The advantage of having a professional fanzine was that you let fans write. There was a variety of voices, people writing about an artist they were impassioned about. It had a super-robust period of '81–'84." Then Dreese came to a realization. "When you're in the printing business, you think

JUDGING AN ALBUM BY ITS COVER PAYS OFF

Gary Stewart worked as a clerk at Rhino Records in the 1970s and '80s before joining the Rhino label in an A&R capacity. During his days in the iconoclastic store, certain albums had an attraction that went beyond the music on the vinyl; the cool covers helped seal the deal. He lists a few.

1. "Any of the first five Roxy Music albums, especially *Country Life*. Probably the first time I'd seen a band keep an interesting consistent cover theme (unless you count Chicago)."

2. **Sun Ra.** "Any and all albums where he did each cover individually (in crayon, I think). I had never heard of Sun Ra before, and I assumed he was just a small local indie artist and the individually drawn covers didn't seem like a big deal, yet I saw many of them cross the counter and now have bragging rights to that story."

3. **Sparks'** *Kimono My House.* "Heard endless hype from *L.A. Times* critic Robert Hilburn and *Phonograph Record Magazine* and never forgot the cover with the two Japanese girls when I finally pulled the trigger on this."

4. **Grand Funk's** *E Pluribus Funk.* "The first record I saw in a round shape (though its predecessor *Ogden's Nut Gone Flake* by the Small Faces is the true classic). Still, I loved what Mark Farner and company were doing at the time. And the shiny surface didn't hurt either."

5. **Captain Beefheart's** *Trout Mask Replica.* "If the title didn't do it for you, that cover was (and is still) unforgettable."

6. **Emerson, Lake & Palmer's** *Brain Salad Surgery.* "I saw this at a friend's house and got to experience its die-cut fold-open cover [art by H.R. Giger], which incited me to purchase it (after hearing "Karn Evil No. 9" on many a FM radio station). Still one of the great (and greatly maligned) progressive albums of all time."

you are in the rock business and you find out you are in the advertising business. Eventually you are in the collections business and that's the worst business to be in. Bar owners would get four or five months behind and then stiff you."

Outside Washington, D.C. in Maryland, Yesterday and Today Records became a hang-out for the city's punk groups before store owner Skip Groff started producing bands for Dischord and running his own Limp label.

Henry Rollins calls it "the most important record store in my life." Crammed with vinyl, posters, and flyers, Rollins said, "It was a record-store-lover's record store. Skip had albums but the emphasis was on the single, Skip's favorite. He once told me that a band puts everything they have into those two songs, so it's always the single you want to pay attention to.

"When I became more familiar with the routine of the single-off-the-album with the non-LP B-side, different picture sleeves for different territories, that was it—I was a singles fanatic. Skip went on buying trips to England and I would often be at the store, sometimes before it opened, to have the first crack at all the things he had brought back. I still have almost all of these singles and many of them are now worth a lot of money. There was nothing like being able to buy the Damned's "Neat Neat Neat" single for $3.

In 1979, Foos and Bronson sold the Rhino store to focus on the label, "which was the time the students came in," Stewart said. In the 1980s, the Rhino store became a haven for world music, breaking acts such as King Sunny Ade. Ry Cooder shopped there. And a slew of musicians started to work there, among them Steve Wynn, leader of Dream Syndicate, who would go on to a successful solo career; Nels Cline, the experimental guitarist who would join Wilco; Sid Griffin, leader of the Long Ryders and an author; and Greg Dulli from The Afghan and Twilight Singers.

"Working at Rhino was like going to college," Wynn said of his stint there from 1980 to 1982. "The stuff that was coming out—the English folk music, the free jazz, the reggae, the dB's, Robyn

Yesterday and Today was a significant record store for the Washington, D.C., punk scene.

Guitarist Nels Cline was a clerk at Rhino Records in the mid-1980s.

Hitchcock—I made it my mission to force it down people's throats. It was a pretty snotty little store. But I couldn't do that, be in cantankerous asshole mode all day."

The types of artists who had been the foundation of stores such as Rhino— the Go-Go's, the Police, and the Clash—were having mainstream success until the definition of a hit was rewritten by Michael Jackson's "Thriller," which spent 37 weeks at No. 1, Bruce Springsteen's "Born in the USA," and Prince's "Purple Rain."

Those multi-million sellers helped make Newbury Comics one of the phenomenal success stories of the 1980s. From 1983-89, it grew 80 percent a year as the business went from $2 million a year to $30 million a year. It increased one store a year until it had 28, and the typical store grew 50 percent per year in terms of income.

When Tower put an enormous store in downtown Boston, "we were safe because we were already in the suburbs," Dreese said. They would advertise: "Don't pay Tower-in prices."

Perfect Sound Forever

As important as the hits was a new format that helped fuel the growth of music sales in the '80s—the compact disc.

Lee Cohen was working for Licorice Pizza when

A promotional display for Bruce Springsteen's *Born in the USA*

he attended a convention for music retailers prior to the introduction of the CD. "They had a big stage and a string quartet playing and beautiful sound. In the middle of a number, a member of the quartet would get up and leave. They did this until there was no one left and the music was still playing. They pulled away the curtain and there was a CD player."

Flash-forward a year and Cohen is at a meeting of a CD advisory group. Sony and Pioneer, which would be manufacturing players, made their presentations saying they would introduce the machines in a few months. "In a year this is what your customers will buy," Cohen remembered. "All the chains had complaints."

Tower's Russ Solomon was concerned about the items being shoplifted, fitting the bins already in place, and, from an aesthetic point of view, the art on album covers. "We had to convince Columbia and Warners to develop the longbox so they would fit nicely in existing [bins]," he said. Years later, environmental concerns had companies

BEHIND THE COUNTER CULTURE

A few of the odd tales from behind the counter.

Musician-composer Ben Vaughn: "A male friend of mine worked at Sound Odyssey in New Jersey and was a real punk fan. One day, this beautiful girl came in and asked for Patti Smith. Immediately smitten, he suavely led her to the Patti Smith section and pulled out several selections for her to consider. She asked which one had 'The Warrior' on it. My friend stopped cold, pointed to the Patty Smyth & Scandal section and abruptly walked away."

Musician Ben Vaughn, 1990

John Kunz of Zebra Records, Austin: "Rhino had released Ruben and the Jets 45s on red, white, and blue vinyl as a Bicentennial record. Wild Man Fischer had been selling a lot at Zebra and they had a special deal—order 25 or 50 of Ruben and the Jets and receive a countertop display. My assistant manager and I were both record collectors and we really wanted the record and the display. We were always setting aside stuff to buy. We figured we could pull this off so we place the order and we get this beat-up, handmade thing that looked like it had sat on the Rhino counter for five years. I always had the impression that they created this offer figuring no one would respond so when someone was stupid enough to do so, they had to scramble and send us something. It probably got thrown away after two weeks. It could probably command a fortune on eBay today."

Jeff Davis, clerk at the Record Outlet, Detroit: "Mitch Ryder came walking into the store. I recognized him because years before, I had seen the Detroit Wheels perform at Detroit's big annual car show, Autorama '67. So I was fairly in awe. He came to the counter, bummed a cigarette off me, and walked around the store smoking it. (That was still allowed in 1976.) A little while later as he's about to leave, I offer him another cigarette, hoping to make conversation. He accepts it and we walk outside together. We lean up against the building and light up. After a few minutes I say 'So Mitch . . . what happened?' He looks away, blows a smoke ring and says, 'I don't know, man, I don't know.' Then he walks to his rusty clunker of a car, gets in, and drives away."

Gary Helsinger, clerk at Tower Records, West Hollywood: "I'm dying to meet Midnight Oil and they're playing a few shows at Universal Amphitheater. *Diesel and Dust* was out and I see the drummer Rob Hirst going to Dukes for lunch. I go over to him and say 'I really want to meet Peter.' Rob says he's looking for Badfinger records. I go to the show and afterward I'm backstage and I pull him aside and say 'Rob told me to tell you I have some Badfinger records.' I brought him the records—and these are the weird collectible records—the next day and he says 'how much' and I say nothing. But I ask, can you play 'Hercules'? It's a weird song and they never play it. I go to the show, first encore, second encore. No 'Hercules'. They do a third encore. They're never gonna do it. He comes out for a fourth encore and says 'I made a new friend today and he just wants to hear one song. Here's "Hercules" mate.' I almost had a heart attack."

Paul Epstein, owner, Twist & Shout Records, Denver: The Beatles' butcher-block cover of *Yesterday and Today* "is the most common rarity in spite of its reputation as being the ultimate rarity. There are thousands of them out there. The first one I bought was a classic example of record store karma. I always figured, even if I don't buy anything, I can make the person feel all right about the whole experience by asking them about their life, showing sympathy for the departed owner of the collection, and then carry the collection back out to their car for them and tell them where the nearest Goodwill is. [In 1989] a lady brought in a huge collection of crap. I mean moldy easy listening, big band vocals, *Reader's Digest* collections. The kind of collection every dealer has seen a million times. I go through what must have been 500 records without taking one out to buy. I go through the whole *magilla* because it is a sweet old lady who I converse with. The last record in the last box is a pristine second-state mono 'Butcher' cover. I pull it out and say 'I'll give you $10 for this Beatles album.' (There are many sides to record-store karma. I've overpaid a few times, and I undercharged many times early in my career but I have underpaid as well.) She said 'If you take all of them, you can have it.' The beginning of a great career."

attempting to eliminate the longbox. Solomon wanted to keep them. "I made a stupid mistake and lined up with the bunch that wanted to hold on to the longbox. Not one of my finest hours."

The presence of the CD forced many storeowners to stock three formats of a title—CD, LP, and cassette. Some of the existing stores drew battle lines early; others have watched the CD lose its value.

"I made a conscious decision that I was a record store and I was a record collector," said John Goddard of Village Music in Mill Valley, California. "I wanted to keep it that way. I had 15,000 titles in CDs and 3,000-4,000 cassettes. I never totally ignored any format. But it never got to the point that vinyl was not less than 75 percent of the business."

Steve Wynn noted, "The downside when CDs started was they wanted to load up 70 minutes of music. That's not how people work. You create in small bursts."

Add to that the assertion of Terry Currier, owner of Music Millennium in Portland, Oregon, that most Americans do not have the attention span to stick with an album beyond 40 minutes.

"Music was treated like art on LP," Currier said. "The CD format was treated by a lot of people like cassettes—they'd throw them around in their car. It got away from being the art and becoming more of a product. The MTV era didn't do us any good even if they learned how to sell albums off a four-minute commercial based on a song."

Stupid *and* clever: Spinal Tap created the *extra* long box in 1992.

By the end of the decade, vinyl would be largely phased out. Tower Records stuck to its guns by offering as much catalog as possible. Solomon estimated the Sunset Boulevard stores had 80,000–90,0000 CD titles and the store at New York's Lincoln Center got up to about 120,0000. Minneapolis, thanks in part to the attention Prince, the Replacements, and Husker Du brought to the city, became a hotbed of musical activity.

"There was no turnover at the cool stores," said Linda Pitmon, a drummer who worked at Positively Fourth Street—"a longstanding hippie store where I was working with frat guys who were into the Grateful Dead because of 'Touch of Grey.'"

Besides Oar Folkjokeopus, out of which Twin/Tone Records was founded, there was Electric Fetus, Garage Door, Roadrunner, Aardvark, Northern Lights, Hot Wax, the Wax Museum, Let it Be, and others throughout the 1980s.

"The more knowledgeable your community is, the more creative they will be," said Pitmon who

Terry Currier munches on cassettes in 1999 for a Save the Cassettes event at Music Millennium in Portland, Oregon.

has drummed with ZuZu's Petals, Golden Smog, and her husband Steve Wynn. "I was such an avid listener and fan, getting exposed to music by these Svengali figures. Just the denseness of that passion, the excitement and knowledge. I would watch people buy records and then make their own records based on what they were listening to. It's a circular chain. I hope it's still going."

In New York, the Music Maze, located in a small apartment house with a basement, closed up shop. Holsapple remembers the next occupant. "The building itself was eventually taken over by

a brothel, operating under the name The Cookie Jar. Unfortunately, when pictures of The Cookie Jar were in the news, all you saw was the glorious neon sign of the Music Maze lighting up the front window."

Twin/Tone Records promoted its artists with compilations intended for in-store play.

THE MOUNTAIN GOATS' JOHN DANIELLE BUYS HIS FIRST LP

"We moved to Claremont, California, when I was eight [in 1993], and I discovered a place called Rhino Records, which was at the time a tiny shack, stocking mainly used vinyl and boasting dark, dusty air," John Danielle recalls.

"My allowance was a dollar a week, and one week in the fifth grade, when I was 10, having spent 70 cents on two new comic books, I went into Rhino to browse through the bins. I had 30 cents; their lowest-priced bin, the really beat-up stuff, was the 23-cent bin. An LP came to a quarter with tax.

"I was really intimidated by just being in the record store. I felt like for sure everybody in there knew more than I did about stuff. So I spent a long time digging through the bin, wanting to both pick something that appealed and something that wouldn't make me look like a joke to the sages at the counter. And then I saw Jethro Tull's *Benefit*. The band name, which I'd heard from a friend at school (Tom Master? Steve Coleman? Probably one of those two), it sounded so hard and harsh to me. And the album sleeve, which pictured the members of the band as cutouts from a paper-doll book on a similarly handmade stage, gave off a comparably dark radiance. I was a little afraid of it; I am attracted to things that I fear. So after long deliberation, I took it up to the counter, and they rung up my total—25 cents. I paid them, and I walked home.

"I played it, and I didn't know what to make of it; I had no idea what the singer was talking about most of the time, but it sounded grown-up. The one song that never left me, and which I still sing to myself all the time, especially when I have to catch a cab, was 'To Cry You A Song.' I meant to learn and record it, but such is the fate of so many planned cover versions.

"The song still conjures, at any rate, and will probably always conjure for me a dusty record store, clearly not yet a money-making proposition, selling records that might or might not be of interest to anybody. Given the right combination of circumstances, they could take root in a young kid's brain and serve, for years, as a source of inspiration to which he could return, continually, like a signpost on a path that might otherwise be hard to find."

CHAPTER 7

THE HIGH NUMBERS

HAVING A NO. 1 ALBUM in the U.S. has meant different things at different times. A No. 1 in 1961, for example, would be based on different criteria than the chart-topper in 1981. And in May 1991, the entire system changed in a way that would affect record stores for decades.

Vinyl albums were on their way out and with that went a way of doing business. Strawberries, the New England record store chain, had a new plan for music retail—a brand new 15,000-square-foot flagship store in Boston that would serve as the company's new model. The emphasis, though, switched to home video from CDs.

SoundScan greets the 1990s by stripping control of the charts away from the labels

> "We were usually ahead of [the charts]. SoundScan had more of an influence on what the big box stores carried. The easiest thing for us was to carry all new releases."
>
> —RUSS SOLOMON, TOWER RECORDS

By the end of the decade, SoundScan had introduced the concept of the No. 1 debut. Since many albums did their largest sales in their release weeks, it amplified the importance of opening strong and rewrote the path that records take at retail. It also redefined the concept of market share and exposed how large a piece of the retail pie the independent labels occupied. But by no means was it an easy sell to the majors.

Ruining the Record Business

SoundScan computerized the collection of sales information at retail record outlets. The SoundScan system was created by Mike Shalett, who owned a marketing company, and Mike Fine, a polling expert who was among the creators of the CBS-*New York Times* poll. A substantial number of major retailers and wholesalers agreed to supply information to SoundScan so *Billboard* decided to adapt its system rather than to continue developing one of its own. Major labels had yet to agree to subscribe to the sales-tracking system.

"We want to do away with the record-store connotation and establish ourselves as home entertainment centers," Mel Wilmore, president and CEO of the Live Retail Group, told *Billboard* at the time.

But on May 25, 1991, the music industry got its biggest jolt when *Billboard* printed its first album chart based strictly on point-of-sale (POS) data compiled by the freshly minted company SoundScan Inc. Label heads were outraged that *Billboard* would drop the methodology it had used for more than 30 years: a tally based on record stores calling in, messengering, or faxing their sales rankings of records to the magazine.

"I went to a meeting with WEA in Burbank and everyone was in the room but WEA president Henry Droz," Shalett recalls. "We were talking about how the system would work and Droz walks in. Mike (Fine) and I stand up to shake his hand and I don't think we got out three words before he walks up to us and holds his index finger a few inches from my face.

"He says 'In one week'—and he's holding his finger like a number one—'in one week'—and now he's pointing at me—'you have single-handedly ruined'—and now he's sweeping his hand across my throat—'ruined the music business.'

"I tried to offer an explanation, but he jumps in. 'Let me speak. One week. Single-handedly.' And he's waving at the two of us. He never gave us a chance to explain, just turned around and walked out. Our mouths were agape."

They received a similar reception when they visited MCA to meet with the label's CEO, Al Teller. Shalett, Fine, and MCA executives were gathered in a conference room. Teller entered, "like a rock star," according to Shalett.

"He sat down, looked at us, and then around the table. 'Let me ask this question,' he says. 'Does anyone here think we're going with these guys?' Total silence. He stood up and walked out. Everyone in the business said they wanted an honest chart. But at that point they had not figured out how to scam SoundScan."

Labels Air Complaints

Record company executives were united in their complaints about the system. Specifically, they felt the chart did not have enough representation from major independent stores, was too heavily weighted toward chains in the Southeast (because they were the first to sign up), and that, ultimately, it would destroy their chances to develop new acts.

After just two editions of the Top 200 Albums charts had been printed, label executives were beefing to the magazine, which *Billboard* printed. Droz, PolyGram Label Group president Rick Dobbis, and MCA Records president Richard Palmese were adamant that the new chart system would hurt black artists and alternative rock acts. Jim Swindel, GM/senior VP at Virgin Records, said *Billboard* "acted irresponsibly by publishing the chart"; Paul Smith, president of Sony Music Distribution, criticized the lack of "the right players," which he believed could be fixed.

Mike Bone, co-president of Mercury Records, appeared to be the most furious, telling *Billboard*, "All my baby acts—Material Issue and the Triplets, for instance—they're all off the charts now, and Shalett's going to come in and try to sell me his service? Kiss my ass."

A listing in the Top 100 often translated into greater promotional spending for an act. The labels had become accustomed to being able to manipulate figures so their priority artists would make it onto the chart. Within a few months, Sony Music became the first major record label to agree to buy sales information from SoundScan. While the SoundScan was initially only responsible for two charts—the Top 200 albums and the Top Country Albums—within a few years, *Billboard* had

SOUNDSCAM

Once the record industry started relying on point-of-sale data to track album sales, the old system of manipulating totals by giving gifts, concert tickets, and meals to store clerks to report a few extra sales went out the window.

That did not mean people weren't trying to turn the new system into SoundScam. During the first Christmas season that SoundScan operated, co-founder Mike Shalett received a call from a label owner concerned that one of his best sellers was selling more than he had shipped.

"We're talking big numbers," Shalett noted. "I asked 'are you manufacturing the CDs?' and he says 'no, we had to ship it out and they gave us a count.' I said, 'OK, I think the math is telling you something.'"

It was a sure sign the album was being pirated. Shalett shared other tales of a few early attempts to bulk up an album's sales:

• The candy bar. A storekeeper put a bar code for a record on a candy bar so that every time he scanned the candy, it registered as an album sale.

• Knowing that independent stores would be assigned a "weight," some less-than-scrupulous owners would call to ask, "What's my number? Am I a five or a seven?"

This referred to the number that would be multiplied by the number of sales to make up for the indies that were not being counted. "But then you would look at the size of the store and realize they were selling too many copies for a store their size. So we threw out all of the sales." The weighting system took about five years to finalize.

• "We were having a sale" was the common response if SoundScan called a store to ask why 20 copies of an album were sold back to back. If there was no other explanation, those totals were thrown out, too.

• Getting a spike for an unsigned band. Here's how that would work: A box of 25 CDs for Band X would be sent to a store. The clerk who unpacked the discs didn't notice that the box was never ordered. A "customer" comes into the store within 24 hours of the arrival of the box and asks for any and all copies of the new album by Band X. Now SoundScan reports that sale of 25 copies of Band X's album. The "customer" takes the box home and repeats this with another store. The sales, if undetected, create a regional blip in SoundScan and an aggressive A&R executive suddenly thinks he has come across an unsigned act that has a healthy following. Alas, they do not.

converted all of its charts that included sales data to SoundScan. It introduced digital sales charts in mid-2003.

SoundScan had its roots in a research project that Fine and Shalett organized in 1989 to present at the 1990 National Association of Record Merchandisers conference. Their project was an attempt to quantify the national consumer of recorded music. The presentation caught the attention of Tom Silverman, the head of the R&B/dance music label Tommy Boy Records. At a breakfast meeting, Silverman offered to hire Shalett as a consultant for the day for one dollar and, as his representative, Shalett would attend a closed meeting with the top brass of *Billboard* and other record labels. The meeting had been called to discuss *Billboard's* plan to use a POS system.

"The very interesting part came during the Q&A," Shalett recalled. "Stan Gorman (of Tower Records) looked at (*Billboard's* director of charts) Michael Ellis and asked 'how much will you pay us for our data?' He answered '*Billboard* has never paid for data and will never pay for data.' The proverbial light bulb went on in my head."

Shalett's logic was based on the grocery store model. They installed computerized POS systems to increase accuracy in inventory control. The byproduct was a collection of sales data that could be repackaged and sold to wholesalers, retailers, and the content suppliers.

Shalett says retailers told him he should create the system and after approaching Fine, the two rolled with it. They went after the major chains, signing up nine national companies (Camelot, Musicland, Music Plus, National Record Mart, Record Bar, Record World, Sound Warehouse, and Trans World), seven regional chains, and more than 25 smaller outlets to supply data for their initial charts.

In the fall of 1990, it was clear most retailers were interested in participating, and that the SoundScan concept was getting a foothold, even if Shalett and Fine were poised to launch with less than 50 percent of the nation's retailers aboard. Their contention was that they had reports from 99 markets, containing more than 85 percent of the U.S. population, and that a complex weighting system devised by Fine would produce highly accurate numbers.

While they were developing the system, a number of players attempted to purchase SoundScan before it ever released a single report, among them *Billboard*, the Dutch-English publisher Reed-Elsevier and its U.S. publishing concern Cahners, *Hits* magazine, and *Album Network*. *Billboard* had a deal that was nearly signed at Thanksgiving; *Radio & Records* magazine took Fine and Shalett to a celebratory dinner in L.A. for a deal that ultimately fell through.

"To make sure of our success," Shalett said of the deal that was finally consummated with *Billboard*, "the chart had to be in *Billboard*."

> "Every day at EMI, we'd get a call that Garth Brooks, MC Hammer, and Vanilla Ice had sold another 100,000 albums. Every day."
>
> —DANIEL GLASS, FORMER EMI EXECUTIVE, ON SOUNDSCAN'S EARLY DAYS

Whole Lotta Number Ones

The first No. 1 album in the SoundScan era was *Time, Love and Tenderness* by Michael Bolton. And not only would the industry know the chart positions, they would also be privy to the sales totals. It would make it clear to all involved that not all Top 10 records are created equal.

Within two months, SoundScan revealed that No. 1 was more of a revolving door than had been previously documented, and that albums were the top-sellers in their debut week. Among the albums to debut at No. 1 within the first eight weeks were R.E.M.'s *Out of Time*, N.W.A's *Efil4zaggin*, Skid Row's *Slave to the Grind*, and Van Halen's *For Unlawful Carnal Knowledge*. *Billboard* introduced its album chart in 1945, which became a weekly tally in 1956. It was not until June 1975 that an album debuted at No. 1, Elton John's *Captain Fantastic and the Brown Dirt Cowboy*. No albums by the Beatles, Frank Sinatra, the Beach Boys, Elvis Presley, or any other superstar ever debuted at No. 1 prior to SoundScan.

"Some label executives got preoccupied with building up first week sales," said Geoff Mayfield, who oversaw *Billboard*'s charts throughout much of the SoundScan era. "The record companies got jealous of Hollywood when they succeeded with big opening box office. Then they ran into the pitfalls—when there is no great first week, there's no great shelf life either."

In January 1992, *Entertainment Weekly* noted that the opposite of what the major labels feared had actually occurred. New acts were making their way to the top, among them Nirvana, N.W.A, and Ice Cube, but they were not the albums that had the heavy promotional budgets.

MC Hammer's *Too Legit to Quit* had the most expensive marketing campaign in the history of Capitol Records. Richard Marx traveled to five cities in one day to promote *Rush Street*. Despite hitting No. 1 in the pre-SoundScan era, *Rush Street* never made it beyond No. 35. A less-financed Capitol artist, Garth Brooks, had three albums in the Top 40 in late 1991.

"In the years before SoundScan, all records looked like a bell curve," Shalett noted. "The new Rolling Stones record would debut at No. 20, then go to 12, then 4, then hit No. 1, and stay for a few

NEWBURY STOPS REPORTING SALES

Newbury Comics stopped reporting to SoundScan for about five years, fearing that Best Buy and Tower could use the data to beat their chain.

"I explained to some indie store owners 'you have handed the keys for inventory control to your competitors,'" said Newbury Comics owner Mike Dreese. For anyone in a niche market, he contended, SoundScan revealed how various independents were keeping their doors open.

"I knew local stores were at a disadvantage. Boston is critical to break a record, just like Seattle and San Francisco." Translation: A sale in Boston was more valuable due to the student population, the thriving club scene, and word-of-mouth potential.

On the flip side, if an act truly did gain traction at a particular retailer that was not reporting to SoundScan, it would hurt that act's chances of breaking through on a national level. Dreese figures his indie chain's absence from the SoundScan chart in the mid-1990s hurt the Mighty Mighty Bosstones, a ska-punk band that sold between 30,000 and 40,000 albums at Newbury Comics outlets that were never reported.

weeks, and then start to fall off. That was not how records sold."

"Record companies had a mentality that they wanted an album by a hot group to rise on the charts, go from 10 to seven to five. But if it drops to nine, they would say 'let's get on the phone and turn the record around.' They would cajole, bribe, do whatever it took to get the record back up. The record goes from nine to seven and they would say 'we saved the record' and call the pressing plant to order more copies even though sales were actually going backward."

Tower Records' Russ Solomon, who now admits he made a mistake in his unwillingness to report to SoundScan when it was installed, said, "We knew *Billboard*'s method was a little phony but it worked. You'd maneuver a record, which made it a good thing in an odd way."

At the end of 1992, the first full year in which SoundScan data determined the top sellers, Garth Brooks and Mariah Carey were the country's top performers. Upon its unveiling, SoundScan demonstrated the popularity of country music nationally; by the end of '92, country was considered mainstream, with three albums appearing in the year-end Top 10 for the first time ever.

Oops, You're Not No. 1

On Tuesday nights, once SoundScan has tabulated all its numbers, the label that will have the No. 1 album in the country is notified. Bizarrely, the Zomba Label Group has been told twice that it had the top-seller in the country only to learn that things change overnight.

The first instance occurred in October 2004, when a special edition of Usher's *Confessions* was released. The label was told, and they informed Usher, who was playing Madison Square Garden that night. Twice he thanked the crowd for making him No. 1 again. But by the time the concert was finished—and a retailer had sent in revised sales figures—George Strait's *50 Number Ones* had been deemed the week's top-seller and Usher came in at No. 2.

The second instance involved a change in policy at *Billboard* regarding the inclusion of sales at single retailers. The rule was changed in November 2007, when it became apparent that a Wal-Mart exclusive was selling twice as many copies as the album that was about to be crowned No. 1.

A last-second rule change made the Eagles' *Long Road Out of Eden* the No. 1 album on the *Billboard* chart while Britney Spears' *Blackout*, her first studio album in four years, landed at No. 2. The Eagles sold 711,000; Spears moved 290,000.

"More than 700 emails poured into my inbox accusing us of being anti-Britney," remembers Geoff Mayfield, who ran *Billboard*'s chart division for more than a decade. "A lot of kids wondered how we changed the rules 11 hours before the chart ran, and I couldn't understand why they thought that was when the decision was made. I realized that my quote in a story that had circulated said we made the decision in the 11th hour. Guess they didn't know that phrase."

Prior to SoundScan, the only determination of how well an album had performed was handled by the labels' trade organization, the RIAA (Recording Industry Association of America). It certified albums and singles as gold or platinum based on the number of units that were shipped to retailers. If a label sent out 500,000 copies of a disc to meet orders, it was referred to as "shipping gold." (Platinum was the award for shipments of one million; double albums/box sets would be counted based on the number of discs in the package.) Liberal return policies among the majors led to a common joke about certain overhyped albums that wound up as flops: "It shipped gold and returned platinum."

A sign of how the different systems registered retail numbers cropped up midway through 1992. SoundScan reported that sales were at the same level as 1991; RIAA reported an 18 percent increase in shipments, suggesting that the business was growing considerably during a lingering recession.

Bob Bell, a buyer for The Wherehouse chain in Southern California in the '80s and '90s, refers to pre-SoundScan charts as "all smoke and mirrors." For the indies, "it leveled the playing field with the majors and provided more reliable information."

That did not sit well with the majors that insisted the SoundScan chart would not be complete until the Tower Records chain signed on. Tower, which had about 35 stores in 1991, was not using a computerized sales-tracking system at the time. But time after time, label executives singled out Tower as the most important retailer in the country. The *Billboard* charts even gave Tower's sales heavier weight than larger outlets.

Billboard and SoundScan took heat until Tower was in the chart. "I would hear it all the time— 'without Tower, you don't have the true world view,'" Shalett remembers. "It's as if music buyers at Tower had different tastes than the rest of the world. . . . Tower didn't get computerized until sometime in 1993. Did they expedite it to satisfy labels to get into the charts? Probably."

Noted Solomon, "We didn't need a chart to tell us what we were selling. Our buyers were local and companies had a direct line to the buyer in the store."

Shalett and Fine sold SoundScan to *Billboard's* parent company VNU in 1998, a deal that was completed in 2001. Shalett continued working there until 2003 and then consulted for two years. In that period, he saw the national sales decline begin, the impact of illegal downloading, the size and scope of legal downloads, and artists signing contracts that said they would be paid royalties based on SoundScan numbers.

"One thing that made me feel best was we showed how powerful the independents were," Shalett said. "After we created this new thing, market share was not about chart positions but it was an actual market share in terms of sales. Independents represented closer to 20 percent of market share. If you asked the six majors what they believed their market share was in 1990 and totaled it up, it would hit 150 percent before you got to the independents. That's how exaggerated everything was."

CHAPTER 8

NEW DAY RISING

NO MATTER WHERE you shopped in the 1990s, you felt like you were on your own. Several chains had consolidated, and the employees were generally not the types with the wealth of knowledge record buyers had come to know in the '70s and '80s. Display space was purchased by labels, making store interiors appear to be identical, and the inventory never seemed to be as varied as it once was, except at Tower.

Music fans craved the independent stores, but with CDs costing, at a minimum, $13, and usually in the $15 to $18 range, gone were the days when you could load up on music for the week and return again the next weekend.

Independent record stores make their marks by filling the niches as the 20th century comes to a close

The last days of Tower Records in 2006.

The indies became the industry's forgotten heroes. They carried grunge records before that genre swept the country; they helped with the introduction of regional acts. Significantly, they attempted to offer an alternative to the chains, which had become more focused on the music that filled the Top 40 charts and less concerned with expanding the musical horizons of the average customer.

"It's a shame," Tower Records founder Russ Solomon said, recalling the shift in record stores during the 1990s. "First you had a large flipping from entrepreneurial people to financial people—it all slipped away from people understanding what they were doing. They kept believing the future is digital and lost track of the physical.

"The shift of the bulk of retail was to the big boxes (Wal-Mart, Best Buy, Target, Circuit City). Record companies were always in control of the retail structure. When the big boxes got into the act, their control slipped away. Once the big boxes were calling the shots and deciding the prices, the real disparities appeared. There were always false prices on the part of companies, but a real price at the consumer level."

Record labels put their eggs in the baskets of a handful of retailers that made most of their money selling appliances, electronics, clothes, and household goods. CDs by popular artists were used to lure in customers and priced below cost. In 2000, the U.S. government eliminated minimum advertised price policies for recorded music, allowing retailers to undercut one another with sale prices.

"It's sort of a joke if you stand back and look at it," Solomon said. "We're selling you a product that lists for $18.98, but if anyone wants to buy it, it's $9.98. The record companies caved in."

With the introduction of the SoundScan system, the record industry became instantly obsessed with numbers. For the first time, there was a direct correlation between a place on the charts and the amount of money a company was making. Record stores needed to diversify to compete, and the first place they turned was toward selling used items. Every retailer active in the 1990s says the margins on new products were too small to survive alone on those sales; used CDs, records, and cassettes provided a buffer that allowed chains and independents to keep their doors open.

And once the Spice Girls, boy bands, and teen idols hit the charts toward the end of the decade, record stores were suddenly thrust into an arena that was decidedly uncool. It forced independents to not only create an identity, but a separate reality that largely ignored the booming pop business.

Hale Milgrim—who ran Capitol Records when Bonnie Raitt experienced a career revival, MC Hammer became an international superstar, and Radiohead was signed to their first deal—watched growth and greed play into the decline of the labels and chain stores. He worked in retail in Berkeley, California, in the early 1970s where he saw a unique camaraderie among the various record stores. There was a belief that competition was healthy for all.

The CD era of the late 1980s sent consumers back to stores to replace their vinyl collections

Tower Records was renamed for Capitol Records when the label celebrated its 50th anniversary in 1992.

THE MAN BEHIND THE MIRROR

Tower Records on the Sunset Strip was famous for closing its doors or extending its hours to allow celebrities to shop, most famously Elton John.

One superstar celebrity came to Tower during business hours: Michael Jackson.

"Michael Jackson would come in once a month, usually looking pretty nuts with a wig, sunglasses, and Band-Aids on his face," former Tower clerk Gary Helsinger said in an interview just a week prior to Jackson's death on June 25, 2009. "He'd go into a security booth and look out into the store from behind the two-way mirror. For four or five hours he would watch people shop.

"It took a while to realize, but this was his one chance to see people go about their business. It fascinated him.

"We'd talk to him, and he'd give us autographs. He would be this bizarre man-child and then you got on an adult subject and he turned into a businessman."

while grunge, rap, and country exploded with new stars. But there was a scramble to be No. 1.

"The chains all became stronger and stronger and they set out to eliminate the competition," Milgrim said. "Thinking that just because something is going well doesn't mean bigger is

better. At some point you lose focus. The healthiest thing a store like Amoeba has done is kept it compact, limited the number of stores they have."

Thinking Smaller

Eric Levin opened Criminal Records in Atlanta in 1994, just as a new wave of competition was creeping in via the Internet and the deep discounts at the big boxes. Levin had considerable respect for the firmly established record store on his block, Wax Trax. "Those guys were older with a kabillion recordings. It was never a conscious decision to be different."

The distinction that needed to be made, Levin asserted, was between Criminal and the department store. "If I were a label wishing for success at Wal-Mart, it's not going to be a success here. If it's about *American Idol*, that's stuff we don't care about. What the industry lost sight of is that the digital audience wasn't a captured audience anyway. There's plenty of niche left."

Rand Foster opened his Fingerprints store in 1992 in Long Beach, California. A friend sold him a classic rock collection and a guy who had worked in radio sold him a healthy number of promotional CDs. He ordered what he felt were 2,000 essential CDs. While setting up the store, a passerby asked him if he would be carrying any CDs by Juan Luis Guerra. He thought the easy answer would be yes. When the guy returned prior to the opening and

Eric Levin (left) opened Criminal Records in Atlanta in 1994. He is pictured with Doug Wiley from RED Distribution.

in San Diego and found that "toy designers are the new rock stars." He half-joked, "the kids had that same look (of astonishment) on their faces that I did when I was waiting to see Pat Travers and get an autograph."

Niche became a buzzword in the 1990s in entertainment—television had success with quirky shows, indie films became box office hits, and alternative rock, rap, and metal found places alongside the chart-toppers from mainstream country, pop, and R&B.

Clifford Antone founded Antone's Record Shop in 1987 to sell albums by artists that played Antone's club, as well as blues legends. The Austin, Texas, store was firmly entrenched in the blues, appealing to older customers.

asked again, he knew he was not only going to be a curator.

"It's a neighborhood store and it has to service the neighborhood," Foster said. "It's as much a town of neighborhoods as it is a beach town or a college town."

Servicing the neighborhood meant bringing in racks of collectible designer toys, comics and other books, clothing, and posters. Cult items. Foster attended the annual comic convention, Comic-Con,

Rand Foster opened Fingerprints in Long Beach, California, in 1992 as a neighborhood record store.

The interior of Antone's Records in Austin, Texas

"He wanted his store to reflect that passion and it continues to do so," said Eve Monsees, a co-owner of Antone's Record Shop.

After a nearby Tower Records closed, Antone's started to attract younger customers. Add to that Clifford Antone teaching a class on the history of rock 'n' roll at the University of Texas, and the place went through a considerable change.

"A lot of his students started coming in asking for CDs by artists like Magic Sam and Howlin Wolf, which was really cool," she said. "Kids would come in who we would expect to ask for something like Incubus and ask for Muddy Waters instead."

Alternative Rock Softens

Rock music that sold well was in a period of transition as Nirvana and U2, big sellers of 1992, had given way to a more pop-oriented world in 1993 and '94. The Counting Crows, who debuted in 1994, started to revive interest in mainstream pop-rock that recalled the music of the late '60s and '70s.

Atlantic Records released Hootie & the Blowfish's *Cracked Rear View* in July 1994, but it would not take off until the end of the year, eventually becoming the top-selling album of 1995 after spending 55 weeks in the Top 10 and selling more than 10 million copies. Jewel's *Pieces of You*, another debut album, was released in February 1995 and would take even longer to blossom; it was the fifth bestseller of 1995. It sold 9 million.

Ron Shapiro took over as Atlantic Records' West Coast general manager in 1994, becoming general manager of the label's entire operation in 1995. "It was huge counter-programming," he said. "They were all singing about good times and love in a basic human way. It all sort of tied in to (President) Clinton taking office."

The acts were promoted first regionally at independent stores and small chains: Hootie in the Southeast, Jewel in San Diego. The same approach would be taken in late 1996 with Matchbox 20 and their label debut *Yourself or Someone Like You* in Birmingham, Alabama.

"The tipping point would come some time between nine months and two years of regional work. We watched it go like wildfire when the albums would catch on at Wal-Mart and Kmart."

Peter Holsapple, who was part of Hootie & the Blowfish's touring band, got a job at a Borders in Metairie, Louisiana, after a Hootie tour ended.

"It was all pretty much compact discs," he said. "Deep catalog, nice atmosphere, free coffee all day long and proximity to the restroom made it pretty much a dream job. My general managers knew they were dealing with a musician, and much leeway was once again heavily ladled in my direction.

"I decided to be the ace sales guy at Borders, especially at Christmas when I'd pledge to get customers buying at least half again as much as they'd planned on walking out the door with. Of course, with Borders, you had to be able to sell books and Cliffs Notes and graphic novels and brew a cup of espresso as well as pump up the latest Son Volt release.

"It was a lot like a record store there, but the corporate aspect of things, like Grammy endcaps and merchandising and the like, wore thin for me. I loved the autonomy of the little indie stores; about as corporate as we'd get was acknowledging record reps who wanted us to list certain titles when we reported to *Billboard* on Monday mornings. Borders would let you put

"To me it was always more important to have every Bob Marley CD rather than *Legend* and two Bob Marley coffee cups."

—JOHN BRENES, OWNER, MUSIC COOP, ASHLAND, OREGON

GOING SHOPPING WITH MATTHEW CAWS OF NADA SURF

"Record stores have been like a network of living-rooms-away-from-home for me my whole life," Matthew Caws explains. "Playing music is my full-time job, but it feels more like an obsessive hobby made good. I'm just a music fan at heart. If I walk past a record store I don't know, I have to go in. If I know it already, I usually have to go in anyway, just for a minute. I've only worked in two record stores, but those were my first and last jobs, bookending my employment."

When Caws was 11, his best friend's brother let the kids hang out in his room and listen to two records, which they played over and over, *Loaded* by the Velvet Underground and *Rocket to Russia* by the Ramones. "Both of these records ended up being enormously important to me later on, but at the time, they were part of a blurry and powerful sensory overload."

A new kid at school turned him on to the Who's *Tommy*, which sent Caws into the streets to find more music. "I found a listing for Revolutions, on 61st and Lexington, in the *Yellow Pages*. I walked the twenty blocks downtown and found myself in another world. There were rows and rows of records, a head shop in the back, and the smell of incense and T-shirt iron-ons in the air. The Who had so many albums. Better get the one with the earliest copyright date on it first. This store was mystery upon mystery. Who are Led Zeppelin? Is that a pipe? I brought the first Who record home and lost my mind."

At 15, Caws entered Tower Records for the first time. "That yellow and red sign always gave me a rush of excitement and impending guilt; the former for obvious reasons, the latter because I soon became incapable of displaying fiscal responsibility in the face of a record that I was curious about. In my college years and later, the likelihood that I would be eating rice and beans for dinner was usually in direct proportion with the growing size of my record collection." He loved the enthusiasm and occasional sweetness of the employees.

At the cramped Record Runner on Cornelia Street in the West Village, the walls and ceiling were covered in singles and posters: Television, Patti Smith, Dylan, Richard Hell and the Voidoids, the Byrds, Lou Reed, Bowie, T-Rex, all held in place by pushpins.

"Two girls were talking to the man behind the small counter about an upcoming Hoodoo Gurus show."

The store owner, Michael Carlucci, "quickly became a sort of mentor to me, taking an interest in my group the Cost of Living and helping us get on our first record, a compilation of local acts called *Eastern Shores*. . . . After a couple of months, I began tending the store myself when Michael was away on tour with his band Winter Hours. When I wasn't hurting for cash, I'd pay myself in singles. Best job I ever had. Someone whose name I can't remember bought it and named it Hideout Records. A couple of years later, Michael bought it and re-named it Subterranean. For two decades, I never went near the West Village without dropping in. It closed in 2008."

up Clash and Johnny Cash posters, but sales and charts and placement in the store were dictated by headquarters in Ann Arbor."

Holsapple spent five years there before returning to performing with Hootie & the Blowfish. "I could also see the writing on the wall, as the real estate in the store devoted to music was beginning to recede, replaced by accessories and DVDs."

Battling the Big Boys

Borders and other hybrid stores posed a threat, but strategies abounded. In Phoenix, Arizona, Kimber Lanning from Stinkweeds says she did what came naturally to her. "I have made a career of being one lap ahead of the competition. I have always sold things that will be popular a year later." Case in point: Green Day.

"We were selling boxes of the first two Green Day albums on Lookout! The band did incredible and the (local) shows were packed. Right when *Dookie* is coming out, some intern from Warner calls my store and says 'we'd like to know if you've heard of this new band Green Day.' I laughed. The more popular they are, the less we sold. That's okay. I can sell 30 Crumpskine 7-inches in the same time as two Warner Bros. CDs."

"The important part of retail is the culture you're selling," Rand Foster of Fingerprints noted. "It's the museum element that stimulates people."

Schoolkids in Ann Arbor, Michigan, was able to compete with a Tower Records in the college town, but it was a Borders that posed the biggest threat. Owner Steve Bergman continued to carry vinyl and became the only store in town to do that. "We were at our most profitable because we could sell it at list price."

Competing by just selling music was difficult. Storeowners felt the need to have vinyl, CDs, and cassettes as they watched stores that favored only

THE SOUNDS OF AUSTIN

Each March, thousands of musicians, journalists, industry folks, and fans descend on Austin, Texas, for the South By Southwest music festival. In October, another massive infusion arrives for the Austin City Limits Festival.

Friends with organizers in the festivals—two of the most significant annual music events in the country—Waterloo Records has played a significant role in both, especially as a conduit between fans and performers.

SXSW has become known for scheduling live music from mid-day until the wee hours of the morning. For the first six years, there was minimal music in the daytime.

"In March of 1993, kind of at the last minute, we did an in-store with Robyn Hitchcock, Mike Mills (of R.E.M.), and Jules Shear. This was way before all the day parties," said John Kunz, Waterloo Records' owner.

"In the beginning of doing in-stores for SXSW, it was always with Texas bands that didn't get accepted. We owed it to the folks who came [to hear Texas music]. Politics got involved and we put together a committee of people with varying tastes to determine who will play in the 15 slots we have during the week. We get about 100 submissions and have a nice cross-section."

Kunz was involved in the Austin City Limits Festival since it began in 2002. "The vision was that they wanted the festival [to display] the best things Austin has to offer. It's a chance to market the city."

Between one-third and half of the performers do signings at the Waterloo tent, sharing stories and posing for photographs with enthusiastic fans. "There are a lot of opportunities to meet artists. When you get to meet one of your heroes, it's real hard not to make an idiot of yourself."

John Kunz (right) of Waterloo Records with Willie Nelson in 2009

one format put up "Must close . . . final sale" signs. A CD-only store in East Lansing, Michigan, closed and Schoolkids bought their stock, allowing them to cut prices at the Ann Arbor location. But it didn't last. The store had to move to a smaller, basement location in 1998 and eventually went to an online operation about a decade later. It happened across the country.

"I still haven't gotten over Platterpuss in Santa Monica closing," said musician-composer Ben Vaughan. "Or Phi Beta in Studio City. Or that place on Venice Boulevard, near Centinela. I always felt that used record stores are like museums. Time does not exist if the curating is well done."

CDs and cassettes were firmly entrenched as the formats of choice in the 1990s, spawning a new breed of store: the lifestyle store. Not everyone was willing to succumb, but in the '90s, the record store chains opted to cut into shelf space formerly dedicated to music and bring in DVDs, trinkets, and band merchandise. The independents had to decide how to compete.

One answer was diversification. "You're not lowering yourself by selling a Jonas Brothers sweatshirt," said Newbury Comics CEO Mike Dreese. "It's what the customer wants. [Independent stores] couldn't exist the way we did when we started. It became snob-based not fan-based. But the people in the indie community who became the winners were the quirky ones, the ones who worked hard."

Essentially, it was the boutiques that made shopping a combination educational trip and treasure hunt. "Aquarius is a great model for a boutique store—but it does require heart and soul," said Marc Weinstein, co-owner of Amoeba Music. He applauded the extensive critical writing reviews published on the Web site of Aquarius, which opened in San Francisco in 1970 and continues to carry an astounding array of offbeat music.

"The online sales are good enough to make it work. I make a habit of going to Aquarius to buy records. Love to see what they're highlighting. I love that experience."

Three Fascinating Boutiques

The 1990s saw the opening of three significant boutiques whose inventories would come to define various sub-movements in music. Through careful curation, impressive press clippings, solid Internet presence and mail order, and personal relationships with dozens of labels and musicians, the three stores outlasted Virgin, Tower, and local chains. They did so against heavy odds, Tower's Solomon pointed out: "Retail storefronts paid unrelenting high rents that rose every year through the 1980s and '90s."

Dusty Groove opened a weekends-only physical location in Chicago in 1997 after a year of operating as a Web-only retailer specializing in jazz, R&B, foreign soundtracks, and music

New York's Other Music has become a crucial outlet for independently released music.

Chicago's Dusty Groove specializes in jazz, R&B, soundtracks, and music from Brazil, Africa, and Europe.

from Brazil, France, and Africa. Downtown Music Gallery opened in lower Manhattan in 1991, dedicating itself to the avant-garde, whether jazz, folk, rock, or classical. And in the East Village, Other Music became New York City's store of choice for various scenes after the three music buyers at Kim's Underground opened their own place in December 1995.

"People love to come in to get something they haven't heard before," said Other Music co-owner Chris Vanderloo. "It's amazing how open people are in New York with their ears and their wallets. They're totally into new stuff.

"It's interesting to watch people from labels pick up imports and obscure stuff, and a year later you see all of it on domestic reissues. Beck would buy tons of stuff and then you could hear [those influences] in his next record."

Musicians helped attract business to Dusty Groove as the store was a key supplier of CDs and used vinyl when Brazil's Tropicalia movement was revived by the likes of Beck, David Byrne, Saint Etienne, and Stereolab.

"Tropicalia was very good to us," said Dusty Groove's head buyer and co-owner Rick Wojcik. "We were selling bossa nova and because the indie rock press like *Spin* would say this is hip, we'd do well. Blue Note Records and soul-funk were doing equally well but whatever is in vogue, contemporary soul singers say, people seek it out, and search engines like Google have been very good to us, too."

Dusty Groove, to hear Wojcik tell it, is the result of a fluke. He was a fanatic record buyer and collector who would travel overseas and pay for his trips by bringing over records to sell. The business was started as an online enterprise, then open on weekends and, after five years, opened as a small full-fledged store in the south Wicker Park area.

For the first two years, none of the three principals took salaries. Wojcik was a radio DJ working on his doctorate. His dissertation was on the used record marketplace with plenty of "high theory economics of value, the exchange of memory. Putting things into quantifiable terms—why one record is worth $5,000 vs. a $2 record."

He wrote 100 pages and walked away. Obsessed with records, he was unsure where to take his knowledge and skill set. Radio was not the answer, he decided, and teaching was not as fulfilling as he thought it might be. "When you work behind the counter, you see that people look at music in a different way. We're always committed to music that falls through the cracks."

Downtown Music Gallery handled the distribution of John Zorn's Tzadik label and offered

"As a young man, I was always going into record stores and listening to the clerk. I learned I liked to listen to what people had to say about what they liked. Being at retail, you have to use your ears as a survival tool."

—RICK WOJCIK, DUSTY GROOVE

the world's best selection of experimental music and free jazz by artists such as Fred Frith, Anthony Braxton, and William Parker.

"We were selling tons of indie rock at [Manhattan video store] Kim's, and when we first opened, Pavement was king, you had Unrest, Liz Phair," said Other's Chris Vanderloo. "It waned as everyone got tired of listening to Lou Barlow.

"At the end of '95, post-rock had started—Tortoise's second album came out three weeks after we opened. Then Krautrock blew up. We couldn't get enough. Then we had a free jazz era, Superchunk's Wobbly Rail, Thurston Moore.

> "There's nothing better than connecting with a customer. It's a rush when they come back two weeks later and say they love something you recommended."
>
> —CHRIS VANDERLOO,
> OTHER MUSIC

Tinariwen from the southern Sahara desert is among the many artists who have performed at Other Music in New York. This in-store was in 2007.

We would dabble in it at Kim's and then it was really hot for a while. Then Aphex Twin, Mouse on Mars, Carl Craig, and Chemical Brothers took off.

"Indie rock, which was played out, is king again. Now that there is no Tower any more, what we were doing when we opened has become mainstream. We're still not used to this—Grizzly Bear in the Top 10, Animal Collective, Top 20—that stuff is our top sellers along with great '70s African reissues."

Unlike Other Music's East 4th Street location, Downtown Music Gallery has moved around New York, starting on Fifth Street in 1991, moving to the Bowery for six years, and then to Chinatown in March 2009.

DMG founder Bruce Lee Gallanter started working in record stores in 1978 in New Jersey, handled jazz at the Record Hunter for a few years, worked for the import distributor Jem, and eventually wound up working for the man who would become his partner in DMG, Manny Maris. With a few partners, Downtown Music Gallery was opened in 1991 and after four or five years, Gallanter took over the shop by buying out his final partner for $140 per week, paying him weekly for nine years.

Throughout those years, Gallanter stayed active as a presenter of live music, doing festivals with punk bands in New Jersey in the 1980s, and then assembling shows at New York's Knitting Factory, Tonic, and Bowery Poetry Club. After Tonic closed, musician John Zorn opened the Stone, which booked artists whose records were carried by Downtown Music Gallery.

"I was a big fan of the Canterbury sound and I went to England for four months in 1975 to interview members of Hatfield and the North, Henry Cow, and Soft Machine," Gallanter said. "People like Steve Hillage, Fred Frith, Hugh Hopper—and we maintained friendships.

"Manny approached Zorn about a year after he opened the Stone, and he says 'how about you guys curate a month of shows?' It had always been musicians curating the schedule. I said 'let's take this seriously and get some really heavy people to play.'"

Gallatner, Maris said, "has kept alive the spark of the joy of all music. . . . We go out of our way

Leading voices in New York's avant-garde jazz scene, such as Oliver Lake (right), with Michael Blake (far left), and Kreston Osgood, make regular appearances at the specialty store Downtown Music Gallery.

with labels to do business directly with them, directly with artists. To be successful you have to keep establishing contacts with new vendors . . . to keep a store looking like something you have not seen somewhere else. . . . Prince likes to shop in private so he asks if he can come in after hours and we keep the store open for him. Billy Bob Thornton brought two suitcases the last time he was here and we had to go to a secondhand store to buy him a third."

STORES AND THEIR LABELS

Several record stores continued the tradition of legendary shops of the 1940s and '50s by creating labels to release new recordings as well as reissues. Here are a few.

Amoeba Music: The label was put on the back burner in 2008 after the release of five compilations, a Gram Parsons live double-CD set, and studio records from swing guitarist Stephane Wrembel and singer Brandi Shearer.

Antone's: Started in 1987 by club owner Clifford Antone, the label issued records by James Cotton, Doug Sahm, Toni Price, and Memphis Slim. It was brought under the Texas Music Group umbrella in 2006.

Aquarius: The first American new wave label, 415, was founded in 1978 in the back of Aquarius Records by Aquarius owner Chris Knab, Howie Klein, who would become a top executive at Reprise and Sire Records, and record collector Butch Bridges, who would sell out after a year. Initial releases were EPs; among its top-selling acts were Romeo Void, Translator, and Wire Train.

Downtown Music Gallery: In December 2006, the owners of DMG were asked to curate a month of programming at John Zorn's performance space, the Stone. They have released two CDs from those concerts on the DMG Arc label with the goal of doing more including a four-CD set of a Henry Cow reunion. Also, they have reissued two records by Curlew and Last Exit's *New Works.*

Dusty Groove: Focusing on reissues only, the Chicago store had released about two dozen titles by mid-2009 that included Brazil's Jorge Ben, jazz organist Reuben Wilson, and various soul singers.

Ear X-tacy: Owner John Timmons helped finance a fair number of local bands' recordings before creating Ear X-tacy Records, which releases albums by Louisville, Kentucky-based artists. By 2009, he had released 54 albums and 10 of them had broken even or become profitable. The top seller was *Soul Season* by the late Tim Krekl.

Oar Folkjokepus: Peter Jesperson was manager of the Minneapolis store when, in early 1978, he formed a partnership with engineer/producer Paul Stark and Charley Hallman, a sportswriter and rock critic at *The St. Paul Pioneer Press.* The label was Twin/Tone Records. Between 1978 and 1998, they signed 35 bands, among them the Replacements, Soul Asylum, the Jayhawks, Jonathan Richman, and Babes in Toyland. They also distributed records on 20 other labels.

Rhino: Founded by Richard Foos and Harold Bronson, the label started by issuing 45s. It became a reissue specialist beginning in 1978 with a compilation of music by the Turtles. While doing reissues, the label also released new material including an album by Billy Vera and the Beaters that generated a No. 1 single. Foos and Bronson sold half the company to Time Warner in 1992 and the other half in 1998.

Schoolkids: The Ann Arbor, Michigan, store started a label in 1992 and released CDs by local acts and others such as the Kingbees, NRBQ co-founder Steve Ferguson, and Essra Mohawk; the label also did reissues of titles by Bill Haley, Al Downing, and others.

Waterloo: Storeowner John Kunz, singer-songwriter Robert Earl Keen, and Heinz Geissler, an exporter of rock 'n' roll books, formed Watermelon Records in 1989. Keen sold out two years later. The indie released 10 to15 albums a year by local artists such as Alejandro Escovedo, Tish Hinojosa, and the Derailers until being absorbed by the Texas Music Group in a Chapter 11 reorganization at the end of 1998.

Wax Trax!: Originally a store in Denver, owners Jim Nash and Dannie Flesher moved to Chicago in 1978 where Wax Trax! Records became the city's primary outlet for new wave, punk, and, eventually, industrial dance music. The label started releasing singles in 1980, and would later put out early albums by Ministry, Front 242, Meat Beat Manifesto, and My Life With The Thrill Kill Kult. It went bankrupt in 1992, but continued to operate as an imprint within TVT Records.

INDEPENDENTS' DAY

AMOEBA MUSIC opened its doors in November 2001, changed Los Angeles, and, in the process, the profile of what a record store would become. Most would say for the better.

In March 2008, *Los Angeles* magazine set up an NCAA basketball-style tournament that would pit 64 establishments and elements in the city against one another until there was a single champion. Amoeba won. To get to the championship—this was determined by readers' votes—it had to top some established institutions: Grauman's Chinese Theater, In-N-Out Burger, Disneyland. In the finale, Amoeba crushed L.A.'s "Weather."

Amoeba births the indie superstore as the Internet takes its toll in the new millennium

"At this point, Amoeba is the greatest store in the U.S.," said Lenny Kaye, guitarist in the Patti Smith Group and an avid record collector. "They have it all and enjoy it all. I like specialty stores, but this is like a record flea market. There's participation in the culture."

Amoeba opened the doors with 300,000 used records and another 300,000 used CDs in stock, not to mention new CDs and LPs, videos, posters, and memorabilia. The store at Sunset and Cahuenga in L.A. sells more than a million "pieces" a year, year after year, for annual sales of more than $25 million.

"Philosophically we align with every other independent store," said Marc Weinstein. Weinstein managed San Francisco's Streetlight Records for seven years before opening the first Amoeba in Berkeley in 1990 with his friends Dave Prinz and Mike Boyder. "There's a mutual respect but we're a different animal."

Within its first five years in Los Angeles, all of the general-interest record stores had disappeared, as the Tower and Wherehouse chains shut down and the significant independents called it a day as well. Credit—specifically too much of it—was usually the downfall. Tower had flopped internationally except in London and Tokyo, which affected its demise domestically. The Wherehouse got caught up in a series of convoluted financial deals that led to its downfall. Other chains merged with one another and faltered until the competition

The illustrated back cover of Amoeba's catalog gives an idea of the depth of music and accessories carried at the indie superstore.

became the Internet and the big box retailers. One adversary, the department stores, could not be fought. Cyberspace became a mission of sorts—and not just for Amoeba, as various other independents attempted to find a way to coexist with the Amazons, iTunes, and other dot-coms.

Marc Weinstein, photographed in 2007, co-founded Amoeba Music in Berkeley and oversaw the opening of the Hollywood store.

We always try to put as much as possible under one roof, but we don't have half the records we want."

"Community is the big thing about record stores," said Dave Alvin, the Grammy-winning singer-songwriter. "Amoeba made shopping into a never-ending magical event."

In many ways, the national attention Amoeba brought to record stores made people look at whether their own town had a major general interest store like Waterloo in Austin, Texas; Ear X-tacy in Louisville, Kentucky; Twist & Shout in Denver; Easy Street in Seattle; Wax 'N Facts in Atlanta.

Its size in Hollywood, not to mention its ability to weather the retail storm in the Bay Area, gave Amoeba iconic status. If a record store was larger than life, this was it. Just as media attention had defined Tower as the ultimate store of the early 1970s, Amoeba became the poster-child of a record store in the 21st century.

Unlike other stores, however, Amoeba did not necessarily make people wax nostalgic about how

"The book business was in trouble 20 years ago, and Borders and Barnes & Noble reinvented things," noted Rick Wojcik, an owner of Dusty Groove, a specialty Web site and shop in Chicago. "We have to become smart enough to compete with Amazon and, on another level, independent retailers selling online at eBay."

The vision in Weinstein's mind's eye is that Amoeba is "a lot of stores within a store. There's a reggae store, a jazz store, a real metal section.

The romance of the record store extends beyond the discovery of treasures in the bins. There has been actual love amidst the bins.

"I met almost all my girlfriends in record stores, including my wife of almost 15 years," said Marc Weinstein, a co-owner of Amoeba Music in Berkeley, San Francisco, and Los Angeles.

It makes sense, according to a historically minded record buyer such as Bob Merlis. "Part of the reason you were going to the record store was to see if there were any cute girls and what they were buying. It gave you something to talk about."

Romance bloomed for Cary Mansfield during his three years (1973-76) managing Wallichs Music City in Hollywood. He managed the record inventory; his romantic interest was the manager of the store's ticket agency.

"The first gift I gave my (to-be) wife was a Simon & Garfunkel record," he remembered. "She put it on the dashboard in her car and it warped."

In Minneapolis, Peter Jesperson was no longer working behind the counter. The label he co-founded, Twin/Tone, had taken off along with the label's top act, the Replacements, who he managed.

Meanwhile, in Los Angeles, a Replacements fanatic named Jennifer continued to follow the careers of the band members after they broke up. She also kept her eye on Jesperson, figuring he had the taste.

"I'd heard that Peter was going to be in Los Angeles with Slim Dunlap, who replaced Bob Stinson in the Replacements, on November 7, 1993," she said. "Slim was performing at the

Peter Jesperson (shown in 2009) discovered the Replacements while managing Oar Folkjokeopus.

it recaptured a long-lost vibe. Eddie Gorodetsky
was standing near the dozen-plus cashier stands in
the cavernous Amoeba in L.A when he said "I love
it here." But he had a caveat: "People don't talk to
one another. That's the problem with record stores
today."

A Boston DJ in the 1980s, Gorodetsky has forged
a career producing and writing television shows
such as *Dharma and Greg*, *Two and a Half Men,*
and *The Big Bang Theory* as well as producing Bob
Dylan's satellite radio show. He remains an avid
music consumer who sees the demise of the record
store—and the rise of Internet sites—as curtailing
dialogues about music.

He used an example of two fans who might
have met at a store 25 years ago to see what's new.
"It used to be that two guys who loved 1960 vocal
groups from Cleveland would get together and
someone would overhear them and get their take
on a record. With the Internet, they only speak to
each other—the knowledge is not spread around."

Musician Dave Alvin (shown in 2009) gravitates toward
stores that emphasize a community element.

CLERKS, THE RECORD STORE EDITION

In early 2006, actor Aziz Ansari (*Parks and Recreation*) picked up where Jack Black left off in *High Fidelity* in chronicling the adventures of a pretentious, smug record store clerk.

With Andy Blitz as his sidekick and Bobby Moynihan among the visitors, Ansari spoofed a day at Other Music in New York's East Village. Blitz and Ansari brag about their relationships with members of Interpol and Pavement and Sufjan Stevens, rough up a woman for not knowing about Pitchfork, and ultimately shoot a guy for his use of the word "indie-tastic." The three-and-a-half minute short was part of Ansari's "Human Giant" series but became an Internet sensation.

"Aziz was a customer and he stops by one day and asks if he could shoot in the store," said Chris Vanderloo, one of three owners of Other Music. "We didn't know he was a comedian. They didn't want any customers so we had them come in an hour before we opened.

"They never gave us a script. Next thing I know, the blogs are writing about the video, and people are coming into the store saying 'I saw the video.' It's pretty classic.

"But I did take offense. . . . I have been in stores exactly like that and I always thought we were never quite like that and always tried to not be like those stores. It's hilarious but at the same time had to wonder—is that how people perceive us?"

People show up with lists, plan to spend three or four hours shopping, or else limit themselves to one particular section. Gorodetsky's shopping spree on a summer day in 2009 was heavy on CDs by country artists from the 1950s.

"It's big, but it suggests there is still room for a curated store in Los Angeles," noted Rand Foster, owner of Fingerprints in Long Beach, California, a 45-minute drive from Amoeba.

"What sets us apart," Weinstein pointed out, "is the sheer amount of intelligence and love for 'the product.' Our staff . . . is people who really believe music is the most important thing in their lives. The vast majority of our employees are record store lifers, passionate music collectors. A large percentage are musicians."

Birth of the Indie Superstore

The idea for Amoeba was hatched in 1989. Weinstein had met Dave Prinz in the San Francisco neighborhood in which both of them worked.

Prinz had sold a chain of video stores and had about a year to create his next business venture.

"We mostly talked about the scale of an operation so we could make a good living," Weinstein said. "What could we do that would require less than $300,000? I had to borrow $100,000 to get in. We got 3,500 square feet on Telegraph [in Berkeley] with a big empty space next to us. Within four years of opening we were up to 13,000 square feet.

"[In 1997] we heard about the Haight location and it felt like a no-brainer to open in San Francisco. Oddly, it was politically tough—the residents don't like super-sized stores. Freaks were normally on our side but here they were fighting us because it was so big."

Beginning in 1999, they started to consider entering the Los Angeles marketplace after countless customers from Southern California who had shopped in the San Francisco Bay Area asked why they had not expanded to the south.

Months before it opened, Amoeba came to L.A. with nearly $2 million in its pocket to buy used inventory for the store. Weinstein made house calls in the months before opening, scooping up collections from the homes of record executives, aging punk rockers, and people with no idea of how to deal with an inherited collection. One of those inheritances landed 9,000 unplayed jazz albums from the '60s and '70s in the hands of Amoeba.

They ventured out of town as well, buying the inventory of a store in Chicago, LPs from the Country Music Hall of Fame, and a collection in Detroit that included every Beatles album ever released in any country.

If there was any animosity toward Amoeba's invasion of Los Angeles, it came from the belief that it caused two long-timers to shutter, Aron's, located less than two miles south of the new superstore, and Rhino Records, which was across town on the west side. In an act of record-store brotherhood, when the store opened in Hollywood, it gave shoppers a list with names and addresses of other local record shops.

Aron's opened in 1965 as a small classical music store and grew to more than 9,000 square feet, dominated by alternative bands of assorted stripes.

Rhino's Richard Foos saw Amoeba as another hurdle in a chain of events. "Two bad things that started [Rhino] on the initial downhill run were the (1992) riots and the (1994) earthquake. After both events we went way down and didn't really come back until 1999–2000.

"[That recovery] convinced us to open a bigger store. It was a disaster from day one. Our opening day was Sept. 11, 2001. We went from 3,000 to 6,000 square feet, we're trying to say we're extravagant and six weeks later, Amoeba opens a 40,000 square foot store that dwarfs us. They get the attention, the press. Combine that with the time, with the business softening. We hung in until

Aron's Records, an L.A. fixture for 40 years, closed in 2005, unable to compete with chain stores, big box retailers, and the addition of an Amoeba store less than a mile away.

the end of 2005, but the writing was on the wall from the beginning. If we had stayed where we were, we might have survived—lower rent lower costs—but who's to say? No one else survived."

No Life Records had a short tenure in Los Angeles during the mid- to late-1990s. One of the owners, Mark Kates, said, "the feeling was that there were bright days ahead at the time for U.S. indie rock, though looking back that was wishful thinking. The other and more important factor was that the preeminent Hollywood indie store, Aron's, had become a pretty unpleasant shopping experience. No Life was a real community. Aron's survived No Life, but when the Godzilla Amoeba appeared, it was all over."

Those that did survive Amoeba's arrival either specialized in a genre such as dance music or were located in an area that attracted a mix of locals and collectors, such as Rockaway Records

Four years after it moved to a larger location, Rhino Records closed its doors in 2005.

COMMUNITY OUTREACH

Observations about record stores almost always include the word "community". If there's one thing that they represented in the 1960s and are reclaiming in the 21st century, it's that component of offering a meeting ground. In Minnesota, a record store that had its beginnings during the years of student unrest has reestablished itself at the core of various creative communities.

Electric Fetus, with three outlets in Minnesota, extended the concept of the in-store performance to create a monthly event to celebrate the state's artisanal efforts.

The small chain, which has stores in Minneapolis, Duluth, and St. Cloud, created MinnEconomy, a "shop local" program anchored by a monthly in-store performance by two bands and featuring the food of local restaurants, beer from local breweries, and posters and crafts from local artists. The events, held inside the stores, began in January 2009.

"The economy is tight," said Electric Fetus owner Keith Covart, who credits his daughter Stephanie for pushing the all-local idea. "This doesn't cost us anything except for the work—putting the stages up and coordinating the bands' request. It's better than advertising. We have always had local artists play here and we're always blogging for (other business), but this puts a name on it."

in the northeastern part of Los Angeles, Atomic Records in Burbank, and Freakbeat in Sherman Oaks. Amoeba, though, was hardly the only force working against the independent record stores.

The Kids Stop Buying

Amoeba was becoming the be-all and end-all for music stores in America at a time when the youth of America was enamored of Napster, the computer program that allowed users to share files anonymously and make online music collections accessible.

"A ton of guys were making a ton of money selling bootlegs," said Mike Dreese, the CEO of the Boston-based chain Newbury Comics. "One form of diversification was used stuff. But the dirty secret of Napster was that it eliminated their exclusive as much as it took away their hold on less-expensive CDs."

The major labels and the Recording Industry Association of America (RIAA) would call it stealing and start filing lawsuits against users within a few years; the retail industry froze and wondered what else it could put on its shelves.

"The demise of the record industry began when the heads of the sales departments, the presidents, the chairmen, and the senior vice presidents laid out the groundwork to say the future was in the big box stores," said Howie Klein, who was running Warner Music's Reprise Records in 2001 when he

A LIST FROM THE HALL OF FAME

"The Great Record Stores" was the headline in the Rock and Roll Hall of Fame's 2008 induction dinner program. The list was short, the sentiments deep.

"Nothing else in my life has ever replaced the record store as a focus of musical community, and probably nothing ever will," wrote *New York Rocker* founding editor Andy Schwartz.

After quoting figures that stated 900 stores had closed since 2003, leaving 2,700 music retailers in operation, Schwartz laid out his list of the greatest: Wallichs Music City in Hollywood; Commodore Record Shop in New York; Rhino Records in Los Angeles; Oar Folkjokeopus in Minneapolis; and Bleecker Bob's in New York. Tower was represented with a photograph.

Although not mentioned in the story, Schwartz also wanted to single out the Discount Records outlet in Ann Arbor, Michigan, when Hugh "Jeep" Holland was the manager and buyer. Jeep also managed the Ann Arbor band the Rationals and founded the A-Squared label that released the earliest recordings by the MC5, Rationals, and other bands

A second essay, by disc jockey and Record Museum owner Jerry "the Geator" Blavat, drove home the importance of mom & pop stores in pop history. His list of stores in the greater Philadelphia area included Paramount, Listening Booth, Sound Odyssey, Franklin Music, Platters Ltd., Funkomart, and Third Street Jazz, and ended with a shout-out to a store that was still open, Val Shively's R&B Records in Upper Darby, Pennsylvania, which boasts "over 4,000,000 oldies in stock."

saw this play out. "They would lure people in with cheaply priced music. They would not respect the music, they would take catalog, they couldn't see beyond their noses.

"It went on all across the industry. Ironically, it hurt the independents at first but a number of independents were able to survive. The larger companies were devastated. The people who love to pick up a record and hold it in their hands may be a dying breed, but they're not going to Wal-Mart to do their shopping."

Wal-Mart promptly became an industry leader by signing deals with artists to offer their albums exclusively. It first made a pact with Garth Brooks for his catalog and then expanded by offering new albums by the Eagles, AC/DC, and Journey in 2007 and 2008. All of those albums posted significant sales figures and other retailers got in on the action, but had less than stellar results. Best Buy believed it had secured a coup by bringing in Guns N' Roses' *Chinese Democracy,* but even with a release at the peak buying time of the year—the end of November through Christmas—the album sold far less than a million. Target had a similar deal with Prince that did not live up to expectations.

While Target did okay with a compilation of hits from Christina Aguilera, greatest hits albums by Bruce Springsteen and Tim McGraw ran into public relations problems when they were released as exclusives. Springsteen even went so far as to apologize about getting into bed with Wal-Mart.

John Brenes, who opened the Music Coop in Petaluma, California, in 1975, and is now based in Ashland, Oregon, pinned the demise of chain stores to business practices that dated back decades.

"When records were sold for $1.99, there was some department store underselling them for $1.29. There's always been a big box issue.

"But when the record companies pulled back in 2002, the problems became clear. Nobody had looked at the reality of what they were doing. When a store wasn't making money, the distributor would extend the terms, it went up 60, 90, 180 days. If you're in trouble, and this was true for all the chains, you get money by opening another store."

The distributors would give the new store inventory and not ask for money for 60 or 90 days, provide thousands of dollars for advertising, and

John Brenes (shown in 2009) moved his Music Coop to Ashland, Oregon, from Petaluma, California.

create new cash flow that would be used to pay the overdue bills.

"It's a bizarre way of doing business," Brenes said. "But the record companies continued to say 'this guy owes us too much money. We can't cut him off.'"

The Online Approach

Weinstein noted the Berkeley store was the first Amoeba to see a significant loss in sales as digital downloading took hold. Like so many stores located near college campuses, as students alter their buying habits, one type of store gives way to another. Berkeley, Weinstein rightfully said, was once the Mecca of record stores and when they opened in 1990, they were one of 10 shops in that college town. In 2009, that number had been reduced to two.

"The 'culture geeks' that once dominated the scene there are simply not there," he said.

For Eric Levin at Criminal Records in Atlanta, the Internet is part of doing business. "If anything, it's a way to talk to my customers using Twitter, Flickr. We have posted 200-plus in-stores on youtube.com. Is it worth the time and investment? Who can say. It makes me happy."

In the early 1980s, Dreese ran a fanzine called *Boston Rock* that was a vital mouthpiece for the punk scene in Massachusetts. In this day and age, though, he sees fans making a more direct connection through online social networks, even though the perspective is the same. That magazine flourished because it featured fans writing about their favorite bands "rather than someone smoking a pipe and attempting to be the next Robert Christgau," the dean of rock criticism.

"A Tower of Babel is largely absent from music this century. Everyone's an authority, everyone's an expert. Facebook and social networks are the future of brand identity. You have your own trusted sources of information. If I say there's a cool book you should read to the 10,000 fans who have signed up for our page, that's much more personal than an ad. And much more powerful than a message from Joe in marketing.

"The Web is giving back. We're going to see tens of thousands (of places) with the stature that can influence buying habits."

At one point, adapting to the Internet appeared to be accepting defeat. For the people who worship the physicality of music, an MP3 was meaningless. The sound quality at the standard rate of 128k bits per second was horrendous and it only added to the notion that music had become disposable in modern society.

There were early Internet adapters such as Tower Records and several independent stores that tried to sell MP3s on their Web sites, but none of them caught on the way Apple's iTunes did. The major labels tried their hands at online retail as well and struggled, eventually aborting all their early efforts. No one was able to do what Apple accomplished. But several retailers saw opportunity there, specifically in the niches. The bumps in the road, though, have been both financial and access issues, which troubles John Kunz of Waterloo Records in Austin, Texas.

"It's surprising to me that the majors find a way to work with long-distance phone carriers more easily than someone who has sent them a check every month for the last 30 years," Kunz said, recounting his experience in attempting to set up an online store at waterloorecords.com. "Each label has a different hoop they want us to jump through."

Waterloo started offering digital downloads in the spring of 2009, enhancing their Web site without major label content. Kunz said he enjoyed learning about digital-only releases "that didn't hit my radar. I'm looking forward to having the full breadth and depth while still trying to curate everything that goes into the store."

There's that sound quality issue. He wants to offer a 320k bps rate. "How can a record store whose motto is 'where music still matters' have a format that's compressed mush?"

Amoeba took a different approach, one that was in line with the nature of their store. Go oversized. Offer the out-of-print, the unusual, and the rare. Spend money.

"It's the first time we've had bad timing," Weinstein said of Amoeba's online project. "It's a really scary time."

By 2009, Amoeba had spent $15 million to build a Web infrastructure to hold an extraordinary number of out-of-the-ordinary items. The idea is to make their Web site unique. They digitized 100,000 LPs, tapping into the obsessions of Marc—Sun Ra—and Dave—Louis Armstrong. There are also 28,000 Brazilian 78s released up through the mid-1950s.

They want to host a Sonic Youth bank that includes everything the band has ever released and then some. He has reached out to people who have made music on the fringes for decades,

> "If there are only Internet stores and you're in a band, where will you hang up a flyer?"
> —CHUCK PROPHET, MUSICIAN

the guitarist Fred Frith and the San Francisco art rockers the Residents, offering to house mountains of their unreleased material.

"We care a lot about it and we want to do it justice," Weinstein said. "It's one of the final frontiers for record geeks—a place to look and listen.

"I see amazing potential in the digital realm. Create a museum online and make its pieces available for purchase. We're trying to find a way to make it look good. In trying to build our own Web site, to do it justice, it has to be really big. Who knows what Apple will spend on its next rollout, $50 million? $100 million? What indie can compete with that. Of course, I'm assuming people are willing to pay for music. I still have my doubts."

FIVE DECADES OF RECORD BUYERS

John George has run George's Song Shop in Johnstown, Pennsylvania, since 1962 and has observed that buying habits change considerably. A baseball fanatic who extends his love of box scores to keeping track of everything ever sold in the store, he provides a breakdown of how sales have changed.

The collectors' marketplace in 2009, he said, means "anybody under 50 is buying LPs, over 50 is looking for 45s. That's 95 percent accurate."

In 2009, the store was selling one LP for every three CDs. In 2004, it was one LP for every 13 CDs.

In the early 1990s, he was selling 100 45s for every LP sold. In '09, "it came down to a 6:5 ratio with LPs selling slightly better than 45s."

Despite catering to an audience looking to flesh out collections, he has always been able to sell the hits of the day, even now. He used to tabulate top 40 singles for the store, with the range being 150 copies sold in a week for a No.1 and about seven or eight sales for No. 40.

Owner John George and the "music walls" at George's Song Shop keep the store popular.

"If you're into Picasso and you go to a museum, you could buy a nice print or a postcard, but you know it's nothing like the original. An MP3 is like a postcard that's a vague facsimile of a painting."

—MARC WEINSTEIN, CO-OWNER, AMOEBA MUSIC

CHAPTER 10

VINYL REVIVAL

ON A TUESDAY night in mid-July, 2009, an increasingly gentrified area in Los Angeles near Dodger Stadium is showing signs of nightlife that look more like New York than the City of Angels. It's 9 p.m. Cafes are still open, a slice of pizza is an option, a live band can be heard booming out of an unmarked club. People are strolling along this section of Sunset Boulevard east of Hollywood, known by rock fans mostly for the wall mural that appeared on Elliott Smith's *Figure 8* album cover.

Origami, a store that exclusively sells new vinyl, has closed for the night and moved its operations across the street to a wine and beer bar called El Prado. It's a long thin room; a mirror behind

Demand for 12-inch and 7-inch records gets people back into the stores in the 21st century

the bartender lists the options. There are about 50 people in the place—the next night at the same time there will be seven or eight—and they're all united over one thing. Records.

This is the modern version of a record club, a gathering that's more social than keen on listening, but clearly united by a love of vinyl records. Six people who attended the week before were given the task of bringing in albums to be played, one side per disk. Ranks are broken once a month when anyone who cares to may bring in a 45 and get it played.

On this night, the ninth "record club" event organized by Origami owner Neil Schield, the program is no different than the others—a bit of classic rock, some electronic music and hip-hop. A recording artist who goes by his initials—AM—brought in David Crosby's *If I Could Only Remember My Name* and the Fixx's *Reach the Beach*; the Faces' *A Nod Is as Good as a Wink* hit the turntable first. *Devious Madness* by the drum 'n' bass act Hive made it on to the turntable later in the night as did the Dungeon Family's *Even in Darkness*.

The crowd attracted a handful of hipsters, but most of the fans were locals who know each other from bands, management offices, and former gigs at record labels.

"It gets people excited about the music," Schield said, noting that he has used his Twitter account and blog to document the record club nights in real time. "Using social networking tools brings that sense of community, and we have people following us all over, interacting over records."

A longing for community has driven a fair number of entrepreneurs into record retail in the 21st century. That has been accompanied by an increased interest in vinyl records, both the collectibles and the new albums that are released, not to mention the everyday titles that sat in four-for-a-dollar bins in the late '90s. Acts and labels have capitalized on the trend, among them Radiohead, Sonic Youth, and Wilco, all of which have had wildly successful vinyl campaigns.

Limited-run vinyl editions of 500 or 1,000 copies have become commonplace for artists—7-inch singles sell out the fastest at Origami—and driven up demand among collectors. It has also created new legions of collectors: fans who previously built their collections through downloads.

"The vinyl thing is real," explained Doyle Davis, co-owner of Grimey's New & Pre-Loved Music in Nashville. "It's a niche business, but it's big enough that we're pulling out CD racks to put in more vinyl. People respond to packaging."

Other storeowners across the country agree, many of them giving off a bit of a "whew" considering how much the business had dipped.

Once the resurgence started to reveal itself, John Kunz of Waterloo in Austin said he was among the storeowners who "put a full-court press on labels and distributors to give us more. Once they did, I was overwhelmingly happy and surprised."

Grimey's in Nashville has been a leader in the sales of vinyl records.

The stories of Davis and Kunz were being repeated in stores across the country in 2008 and 2009. With that come the stories of admiration for vinyl—the tactile experience, the visuals, the warmth of the sound.

"With an LP, you take the sharpness of the CD and soften it. Think of the CD as blinding white light and the LP as adding shades of yellow," explained Keith Covart, who has sold vinyl at his Electric Fetus stores in Minneapolis since 1968. "An LP forced you to listen, to gather around with your friends and share. Talk about it. Maybe vinyl is bringing that back for young kids as well."

Susanna Hoffs of the Bangles associates vinyl with very specific listening experiences that too many youngsters have not encountered. "Sitting in my room, holding the album cover, was so personal," she said. "I always liked the closeness of listening in my room on my turntable, getting the whole statement of an artist. I see why kids are gravitating toward that.

"When I think of a great album, like Neil Young's *After the Gold Rush,* it's all about how one song fades into the next. These days there's too much of a disconnect between songs on albums."

Vinyl—and it borders on the obvious—is the format of choice for people who work in record stores. Kunz gives that assertion a firm nod of the head.

"I have always maintained that we have these wonderful analog listening devices on the sides of our heads that don't want to hear zeroes and ones. They want sound waves, a human-size arc. Vinyl is always going to have that place, especially among the people who work in this store. There is still a tremendous romance for the record. When people bring in their collections, they'll tell you about their attachments to records. CDs never had that romance."

MISSISSIPPI DOCKS IN PORTLAND

In the case of vinyl, there is more than one meaning behind the phrase "what goes around, comes around." A man with an idea to run a record store puts his collection of LPs in racks in a stereo repair shop. Within a few years, the repair shop is gone in favor of records only, and the owner has started a reissue label. It was the story of Rhino Records in Los Angeles in the early 1970s and the story of Mississippi Records in Portland, Oregon, in the early 2000s.

Eric Isaacson started Mississippi Records in 2003 with three racks of LPs in a store that was principally a repair shop for amplifiers, stereos, and exotic instruments. Four months after he moved into the space in Northeast Portland, the 650-square-foot store—located on Mississippi Avenue—changed its emphasis.

"It's heavily curated—and then there's a dollar section," Isaacson said. The selection "really depended on what collections had been brought in most recently. Some days we have the best jazz selection and the worst punk records. That has been kind of our survival tool. We don't get stuck on being one thing. We can be hit or miss."

A friend of Eric's, Alex Usimov, started the label to release local music. The fifth release on the label, in late 2003/early 2004, is when Isaacson stepped in and transformed it into a reissue imprint.

"A friend had a store in Montreal—Back Room Records and Pastries—and he found that his blues and gospel sections were suffering," Isaacson said.

They decided to create records by dipping into the public domain to gather recordings.

Their first release was the blues album *Last Kind Words (1926–1953)*, featuring music by Willie McTell, Memphis Minnie, Geechie Wiley, and others. The other release was *What Are They Doing in Heaven Today?*, a collection of recordings made by Washington Phillips between 1927 and '29.

Five-hundred were pressed and sold out in weeks. The records were sold in Portland and Montreal—for $10 apiece, a price Isaacson has maintained.

The catalog quickly got up to 40 titles and included LPs and singles. *I Don't Feel at Home in This World Anymore 1927–1948*, a compilation that included blues, Cajun music, a Greek rebetica, calypso, and gospel, proved popular as did an album from Thailand simply and clearly titled *70s Thai Orchestra*.

"The label attracts a ton of business to the store," Isaacson said, noting they have no Web site and do minimal advertising. A Facebook page for the store was built by a woman in France with no connection to the store; ditto for the fellow in Asheville, North Carolina, who has monitored a Web site that tracks the label's releases.

As the albums became popular with collectors, Isaacson stuck to his guns and kept the press runs small, distribution limited, and the price at $10. "You want to price things so people in the neighborhood can afford it."

Who's Really Buying?

The numbers that back up the vinyl revival are merely a blip in the grand scheme of the music industry. It's less than 1 percent of all units sold: 1.9 million new vinyl LPs were sold in 2008, though this was double the tally of the year before, according to Nielsen SoundScan, which tracks the sales of new music. In the first half of 2009, 1.2 million units were sold—a dramatic increase, especially considering the state of the economy in the U.S. at the time.

Sonic Youth's successful vinyl launch was more a case of the band's label, Matador, using a two-LP set and an LP of a concert recording as the centerpiece of a deluxe edition that had to be ordered prior to its release. In its first month, Sonic Youth's *The Eternal* sold 3,000 vinyl copies, according to Nielsen SoundScan figures.

"There's always a small run for every record I do," said Steve Wynn, the former leader of Dream Syndicate who made 15 solo albums between 1990 and 2008. "At a lot of shows I play, the vinyl outsells the CDs."

Yet one newspaper after another latched onto the story of the resurgence of vinyl, from *The Washington Post* on down, regardless of the veracity of the story.

Jerry's Records in Pittsburgh has become one of the most important vinyl-only stores in the country. If it has something unopened, it's only because owner Jerry Weber purchased a store's inventory and put it on the shelf.

"Every year or so we'd see these guys come through from Europe on buying trips and then they seemed to skip a few years," Weber said, the reason for their absence piquing his curiosity. 'Jerry,' they answered, 'when we started coming here 20 years ago, we would fly to Atlanta, drive up through Pittsburgh, see you, and then head to Philadelphia, New York, and Boston, then fly home.'"

They operated off a master list of 40 stores. In 2009, that list had been reduced to eight. Some of the stores were under new management and, as Jerry repeated their observation, "had gotten ridiculous with the prices." A good 75 percent of the LPs at Jerry's Records are priced at $3 and most of the other 25 percent are under six bucks. The rarer stuff is auctioned on his Web site.

The Princeton Record Exchange, in Princeton, New Jersey, has the reputation of having one of the best vinyl collections from New York City to Philadelphia. The inventory is mostly used and, like Jerry's, it attracts buyers from throughout the U.S. as well as Europe. Even with a stock of 100,000 LPs, *Billboard* once wrote that it has "secured a niche."

At a place such as Amoeba in Los Angeles and the Bay Area in Northern California, vinyl has become a driving force in how a store stays open. Every year since the stores have been in existence—the first one opened in 1990—sales of new and used vinyl increased. The L.A. store opened in late 2001 and soon thereafter sales started to drop in Berkeley. Amoeba's Marc Weinstein figures the three stores have sold more than 10 million LPs.

Much of that, of course, has been used. Few collections have impressed Weinstein as much as those he has found in the hills above the University of California at Berkeley. "Given the history of the city, there's still a lot of interesting used (records)

out there. It's not the volume it once was, but a classical collection from someone in the hills is inventory that never fails."

Boo Boo Records, founded by two friends who sold used records at a swap meet, has expanded numerous times since it opened its doors in 1974 in California's San Luis Obispo County, along the central coast. It grew to 5,000 square feet in the late 1990s when it started carrying DVDs. Like many independent stores, it turned to the Internet to establish viral stores at Amazon, Half.com, eBay, and Gemm. It carries a large selection of vinyl— new and used.

New vinyl became a crucial selling point for independent stores attempting to attract customers who might otherwise go to a big box retailer. The coalitions that service indies—CIMS, AIMS, and the Music Monitor Network—were able to coordinate efforts to get vinyl in sufficient quantities at independent retail stores and give new releases marketing support.

Then again, Terry Currier of Music Millennium has another quip: "It started with vinyl and it will end with vinyl. We're living antiques stores as it is. That's an unfortunate way to look at it."

In the used marketplace, Paul Epstein of Denver's Twist & Shout noted not as many collections of records from 1980s and '90s are turning up. "Four years ago," he said, referring to 2005, "I would have turned up my nose at something like that, [now] even a great quality

"The Wax Museum" in Boo Boo Records, San Luis Obispo, California, features a large collection of new and used vinyl and is also host to in-house performances.

Fleetwood Mac record can be turned around (instantly)."

He predicted a wave of collectibles will be taking form around the rock records of the 1990s. "There's a 10-year period in which vinyl is very scarce. Pearl Jam's *Ten* is an example. The first Smashing Pumpkins, *Gish*, on vinyl is a giant collectible."

But while plenty of new titles are difficult to keep in stock, at Other Music in New York, co-owner Chris Vanderloo said he worries about the price. "I think it's too high. I know it's because of the cost to make them but how far can it go? A new album by a new band is 25 bucks. The perceived value of music has never been lower and the price has never been higher."

Or as Terry Currier put it: "*Thriller* should not be 35 bucks."

> "I personally love to own LPs. Musically, there's nothing more exciting than buying something, holding the sleeve, and reading the lyrics and the notes while you're listening. It's not as satisfying or tactile with a CD."
>
> —COLIN BLUNSTONE,
> LEAD SINGER OF THE ZOMBIES

Trying Vinyl Only

Though vinyl sales have increased nationally, stores that carry only vinyl were springing up in Southern California faster than anywhere else in the country. By going retro, L.A. was again in front of the media curve.

Three stores opened in Los Angeles in 2009 that pinned their hopes on the continuation of the vinyl fetish. One was Schield's store Origami Vinyl in Echo Park; another was a combination record store and barbecue restaurant in nearby Silver Lake called Territory. The third is Vacation in the Los Feliz section, which carries a variety of genres but was dominated by metal when it opened its doors.

A mixture of new and used, Territory BBQ + Records had its grand opening in May 2009 with a collection of records heavily curated by three fans of various "freak" styles. The store was modeled after Rocket Science in Brooklyn, New York, and Aquarius in San Francisco, according to one of the store's buyers, Zach Cowie. During one visit, the used albums on the wall included selections by T.Rex, Pentangle, and the Velvet Underground; among the new stock were LPs from Tee Pee Records, a label owned by Territory co-owner Tony Presedo. Reissues and new compilations were the only new vinyl the store carried.

"Half the fun of this store is selling things," Cowie said while thrilling to a compilation of singles by reggae singer Horace Andy. "We like to display it and move it out. The goal is to sell it to someone in the neighborhood, not to match the price someone paid on eBay."

Many of Territory's employees, even in the kitchen, had jobs at labels at one time. Nearly everyone who entered the store was either a musician, a DJ, a writer, or an artist. Territory closed in May, 2010.

At Origami, the likely customer is a local resident

Territory BBQ + Records co-owner Tony Presedo with Julie Edwards in front of the singles wall in 2009.

or a person drawn to the area by the live music venues within a few blocks. Schield, too, has leapt at the chance to present live music, booking in-store performances weekly. Some acts are initially taken aback by the setup: They have to climb a spiral staircase and perform from a loft space about nine feet above the record store's main floor.

"Instead of buying a house, I did this," Schield said. A former employee at Geffen Records, he caught the record bug a second time while selling his parents' records at a garage sale.

"It was time to become an entrepreneur," he said. "I called some friends in the neighborhood and they pointed me in a few directions. Serendipitously,

> "One of the frustrating things with used vinyl is you usually only have one copy. When it's a reissue, you can say 'this is a great record' and watch it sell and sell and sell."
>
> —RICK WOJCIK, CO-OWNER, DUSTY GROOVE, CHICAGO

when I asked one person about a location, they happened to own the building."

The biggest coup in Schield's first three months in business was a record release party for Sonic Youth. (He was product manager on their *Murray Street* album.) Sonic Youth did a show in New York to promote the album, but the event at Origami was the only one of its kind in the country.

The store was redesigned as "The House of Shifting Plates and Ridiculous Juice." Members of the band provided names of their favorite LPs, and Schield stocked them along the wall with the notation of Staff Picks from Thurston, Kim, Lee, and Steve. A pizza parlor across the street designed a pizza to resemble the cover of *The Eternal*.

"We had 500 people in here in four hours," Schield said.

Meet Me at the Record Club

When Danny Benair worked at the short-lived Los Angeles store Bomp, one of the thrills was being able to listen to the record collection of the owner, Greg Shaw. Benair and Shaw loved singles and since this was the punk era when singles were a format of choice, Benair was in heaven. Weird stuff, he'd say, is his forte, but the baroque pop records he acquired on an early trip to London continued to resonate with him throughout his life.

Benair, drummer in the 1980s band the Three O'Clock and owner of the music marketing company Natural Energy Lab, mentioned the idea of a record club with a secret handshake. The owner of a store in the San Fernando Valley took him up on it.

Once a month, Benair organizes a gathering at Freakbeat Records in Sherman Oaks, California, giving each one a theme. "In some cases you have to defend a genre or it could be as simple as a song you're excited about," he said. "The best records are the ones where you have a back story."

VINYL AS LUXURY

Lexus appeared to have a grasp on how cool vinyl was in early 2009.

The luxury carmaker created a television commercial to tout the state-of-the-art qualities of its navigation system. A driver in an SUV is stuck in traffic and apparently in a hurry to get to his destination. With the flip of a switch, he is able to detect a better route. The buildings that surround him fall away and he has a clear road until he gets to the one building still standing: an all-vinyl record shop.

Using Facebook to alert people to themes and the show, Benair wondered if it could be transported. "I'm all for having people do it in other cities. I really like the idea of socializing about music, using music to bring people together. And by having it in a record store, the good thing is people have bought a record after hearing it for the first time."

In July 2009, the Danny Benair Record Club went with the theme of deceased musicians. About 20 people gathered to listen to music and stories by the famous and the obscure—rockers, film composers, and jazz singers. Music from Janis Joplin, Son House, Klaus Nomi, Nina Simone, Jimmy Campbell, and Morphine's Mark Sandman brought on nods of approval and discussions about concerts, record purchases, and tangential thoughts.

The record club idea elicits memories of parties in basements, hanging out after school, and the earliest days anyone is exposed to music. Some people have made the vinyl revival a chance to bring on wholly adult pleasures.

Butch Walker, the indie rocker whose production credits include Avril Lavigne, Weezer, and Fall-Out Boy, lost his entire album collection—nearly three decades worth of LPs and CDs—when his Malibu home burned to the ground. A couple of years later, he said, "I invested in a really great amp, turntable, cartridge, and speakers, and started buying all the records I loved and getting a lot of new ones. I'm pretty stoked about it now.

"There's nothing better than sitting down with a bottle of wine and getting up every 20 minutes to flip over the record. It forces you to listen to five songs in a row that are meant to be listened to together. There's no shuffle function."

"We don't even have a CD player in the store."

—JERRY WEBER, OWNER, JERRY'S RECORDS, PITTSBURGH

CHAPTER 11

DANCING IN THE AISLES

PAUL MCCARTNEY GAVE a concert in a record store. June 27, 2007 was the date; Amoeba Music in Hollywood was the venue.

It still seems startling to consider that one of the most famous musicians on the face of the earth would participate in an activity generally reserved for up-and-comers, acts hoping for a bit of career revival, or even those who want to connect more directly with fans.

McCartney showed up with his band and played for an hour and a half. "This is the most surreal gig ever," he told the crowd, estimated at 800. His set, which opened with "Drive My Car," included a dozen Beatles songs and only five tunes from the album he was supporting—*Memory Almost Full*.

Performances and autograph sessions add a thrill to record shopping

Paul McCartney's performance at Amoeba Music in 2007 attracted fans from around the world.

"Tears were running uncontrollably down my face the whole time," said Marc Weinstein, the co-owner of Amoeba who arranged the performance. The *L.A. Times* even noted that Weinstein looked happier than any other fan in the room.

Former bandmates were in the audience. Ringo Starr was standing in front of the John Lennon section; former Wings members Denny Seiwell and Laurence Juber were there as were others with Beatle associations—Apple chief Neil Aspinall, Olivia Harrison, Barbara Orbison, Jeff Lynne, and Joe Walsh. Actors Rosanna Arquette and Cybill Shepherd were also in the midst of fans sporting Beatles, Wings, and McCartney clothing.

It's unlikely that anyone would argue there's a higher pinnacle in the realm of in-store appearances. Others have had people talking for a variety of reasons, but in nearly every case, the key component is the rarity of the experience. There's Nirvana, which played Waterloo Records in Austin, Texas, a month after *Nevermind* was released. Pearl Jam performed at the Tower Records in Yonkers, New York, in 1991 on their first national tour. Sire's Howie Klein convinced Morissey to do an in-store—one and one only—in Grand Rapids, Michigan. Nine Inch Nails played to a crowd of 350 in 1991 at Uncle Sam's Music in Lauderhill, Florida.

For the most part, the in-store "is the greatest thing you can do for a relationship with fans," according to Yvette Ziraldo, a longtime Warner Bros. Records sales executive who worked in record retail for years before switching sides. "You can do in-stores for up to a year after a record comes out. People will line up for them."

Nirvana's performance at L.A.'s Rhino Records, for example, became a thing of legend. The performance was filmed by Rhino employee and filmmaker Sam Epstein, but never shown until 2005 when an in-store screening of the 35-minute film was held at Rhino. The band's performance of "Big Cheese" was included on the DVD in the Nirvana box set *With the Lights Out.*

John Kunz of Waterloo Records in Austin guessed right when he predicted big things for Norah Jones after receiving an advance of her

> "The quiet, poorly attended in-stores can be just as special as the jammed ones."
>
> —ERIC LEVIN, CRIMINAL RECORDS, ATLANTA

debut album on Blue Note, *Come Away With Me.* The album was released in February 2002, less than a month before the annual South By Southwest music festival invaded Austin.

Kunz pushed the organizers to book her a good-sized venue and worked to secure an in-store during her visit. Although based in New York, Jones grew up in Dallas and fit in perfectly with Waterloo's emphasis on Texas musicians. Jones attracted not only one of Waterloo's largest crowds for an in-store—her mother and her first piano teacher were in the audience—it was the largest audience that she had ever played before, Kunz noted.

"Usually at an in-store you attract people who are already fans or already have the album," Kunz said. "Not only were people buying two or three

Among the handful of in-store appearances Nirvana made was one at Rhino Records in 1989, shown here from a video by filmmaker Sam Epstein.

Norah Jones performed at Waterloo Records in Austin, Texas, to support the release of her debut album in 2002.

copies each, there were some folks buying 10 at a time. They were so enamored with the discovery of this new artist. By the time (she sold 500,000), they figured we had sold 1 percent of that total. And there were a lot of record stores around at the time."

Artists First

To be successful at in-stores, explained Rand Foster, who has booked hundreds of them at his Fingerprints store in Long Beach, California, "you have to try to not lose sight of the fact that it's artist first, customer second, and label third. It's ultimately about what the artist wants."

Foster had one logistical nightmare when he underestimated the appeal of an act that had released only one record on a small independent label.

"Somebody called to ask how to get to Long Beach from the Burbank Airport. I'm like 'you're flying in for this?'" he recalled.

The artist was Jack Johnson. The performance was Dec. 7, 2001, 10 months after the release of *Brushfire Fairytales*. The store generally held 300 people but could cram in 350; about 800 fans showed up.

"The cops drive up and ask why all these people are there. I explain and he [the cop] tells me he'll

GARTH BROOKS GETS GRILLED

Early in the summer of 1993, the major distributors were putting sanctions on stores that sold used CDs: Any store with a used section would not receive advertising dollars from the labels to support new releases. That policy irked Terry Currier, who at the time had two Music Millennium stores in Portland, Oregon.

"At the time, only 5 percent of our business was used so I thought this was unfair," Currier said. "I wrote a three-page letter and sent it to every label president and VP of sales and to the trade publications. It started a little war, and people in the industry were going back and forth on the issue. I was still looking for something that could go out to the public."

Little did he know that Garth Brooks would supply the lightning rod. Brooks was willing to go a step further than his label, Liberty, and its distributor, CEMA.

Brooks told *Billboard* at the time that he was against anyone who sells used CDs, becoming the first artist to speak out against the practice soon after The Wherehouse chain announced it would sell used CDs in its 339 stores. "If I have my way, we won't send any product to them, not just CDs, until they find a way to compensate those writers and publishers and all involved with the record."

That quote, Currier noted, came "shortly after he said he had made more money than his kids, his grandkids, and his kids' grandkids could use. So we yanked his product. Within 10 minutes we had every Brooks item written up for return. That was on a Wednesday.

"We wanted to invite the public down, and this would be nine days later, to bring their Garth Brooks LPs, CDs, and posters and tapes to a barbecue at the store. We sent out press releases, took an ad in the paper. By Thursday and Friday of the next week, all the media was coming down to the store and by Saturday (July 9, 1993), the podium (at the barbecue) was so full of microphones, it looked like a presidential election."

Currier was in his office doing an interview with a radio talk show in Seattle when one of his employees came up with a novel idea. He would become Currier's manager and take the Garth Buck$ Bar-B-Q for Retail Freedom on the road. They started in Bellingham, Washington, and ended in San Diego, hitting nine West Coast cities along the way.

"We called stores where we didn't know anyone and they'd set up the barbecue and get the media out. At the Berkeley Amoeba, we were on the five o'clock news and that night we went to the Giants game. There were people shouting at us and cheering us on. MTV followed us with a crew. People magazine covered our barbecue in Los Angeles."

The tour ended in mid-August, just weeks before the release of Brooks' sixth album, *In Pieces*. Brooks was sticking to his guns and continuing to bash used-CD sellers, but by then his distributor had relented and allowed the new disc to be shipped to all retailers.

But Currier had made his point. "By the time we got back, all of the major distributors had removed the sanctions."

In 1993, Music Millenium owner Terry Currier organized the Bar-B-Q for Retail Freedom to fight major labels' policy changes.

be back in 10 minutes and they [the fans] better be gone," Foster said.

"We beg with Jack and he agrees to do two shows. I go back outside and now there are about seven squad cars and a helicopter above the store. A new police officer tells me 'I don't want to know what's going on here. I just want it solved. And we'll be sending you a bill.' We explained the solution—everyone lines up, 300 people go into the store, and then into an empty store next door to get autographs. Another 300 people file in and we do the same thing. We get addresses from the people who didn't get in to make it up to them."

Foster got a good story out of it. And better yet, he added, "I never got a bill."

When stores start out, they generally accept any artist who is offered to them. Once they establish themselves, they can get picky. The key is to place the autographs and the photos prominently to give a store an extra dose of credibility.

The West Hollywood outpost of Licorice Pizza was one of the first places in which the Police did

> "Max Roach did a solo drum concert. The Dirty Dozen Brass Band couldn't fit on our stage so they just played outside in front of the store."
>
> —BOB KOESTER,
> JAZZ RECORD MART,
> CHICAGO

a signing. An autographed poster of Feist, signed before she had a major hit with "1, 2, 3, 4", hangs in the bathroom of Grimey's New & Pre-Loved Music in Nashville.

Quicksilver Messenger Service did an in-store appearance at Village Music in the Northern California town of Mill Valley soon after John Goddard took over the place in 1968. "I did that one because one of the guys in the band was a friend of mine," he said.

It would be years before he hosted another one. Even then, he limited appearances to people he admired—Otis Clay, Hank Ballard—or knew—Ry Cooder, J.J. Cale, Nick Lowe, and Elvis Costello, who called Village Music his favorite record store. "It was about booking people who were important to my past," Goddard said.

The owners of Other Music called Yo La Tengo to play their opening. "It was pretty packed," said co-owner Chris Vanderloo, "but that really helped spread word of mouth, along with some write-ups in *Time Out* and *The Village Voice*."

In-store performances did not catch on as a promotional activity until the 1970s and did not become widespread outside the largest cities until the late 1980s. Part of the problem, noted Colin Blunstone of the Zombies, was the touring schedule in the mid-1960s. "We'd be in these package tours and there were six or seven bands doing one or two songs each. We'd do five or six shows a day and never leave the theater. It was hotel, theater, bus. We never got to see anywhere in any American cities."

In the 1970s and early '80s, Southern California became a hotbed for in-store performances and appearances. The Licorice Pizza chain, which had a store across the street from the famous nightclub the Whisky a Go Go, had the Go-Go's, Ted Nugent, and Runaways greet fans in the store, not to mention all the acts that performed at the Whisky and then ventured in. Patti Smith and The Pretenders were among acts that did signings at store openings in Southern California cities such as Santa Barbara and Huntington Beach.

The French band, Phoenix, one of the hottest acts of 2009, performed at Grimey's in Nashville.

James Brown signed autographs at Tower Records in 1980 for the release of *Live and Lowdown at the Apollo Vol. 1.*

Patti Smith perfomed in the Licorice Pizza parking lot in the late '70s.

Over the years, stores have decided to provide artists with the creature comforts of a concert setting. Stinkweeds in Phoenix, when it moved to its fourth location in 2005, built a courtyard to accommodate bands. Music Millennium, in Portland, Oregon, launched a second store—its priority was an open performance space that could fit 600 people. When the store opened, the goal was 20 straight nights of performances; they did 40 in a row.

"We were not getting the meet-and-greets. Those were going to Tower," Music Millennium's Terry Currier said. "Once [the artists and labels] felt comfortable with us, we got them on a regular basis." Currier lists Soundgarden's appearance on the release date of their first A&M album as a key booking. He changed his vacation to catch Steve Earle play in the store and has marveled at performances by John Hammond and Richard Thompson.

The jazz pianist Mal Waldron took the experience to a different level though. "This guy is up there smoking and I figure, okay, he's 77, I'll let him smoke even though it's against the law. It was the first time that I ever saw everyone in the store just stop in their tracks. Obviously there were people who came to see him, but I'm talking about every customer stopping right where they were and becoming quiet. It was just solo piano."

Soundgarden performed at Portland, Oregon's Music Millenium in 1989 for the release of *Louder Than Love*.

The Store As Concert Hall

A few years after Waterloo relocated to its second location, it was able to take over an adjacent building, expand to 6,400 square feet, and install a proper stage and sound system. When Nirvana played there, for example, the performance was atop planks that were placed over a back counter.

With the new showroom installed, Waterloo was able to increase the number of bookings as well as bring in performers with good-sized followings. Ben Harper had contacted Waterloo's Kunz about performing at the store "but we knew we had

to make it manageable and keep the size of the audience limited," Kunz said.

"Fans had to go [through] several steps—we made them jump through a number of hoops. It helped get us the true, uber-Ben Harper fans. There was an unbelievable excitement there. When I got up to introduce Ben, a wave of energy came toward the stage. I felt like I was being blown back like the Maxell tape guy. I wondered if this is what artists feel like when they're onstage. I never experienced anything like that before or since."

The Jazz Record Mart in Chicago moves 20 bins of traditional jazz out of the way during the city's

> "Lyle Lovett drew about 12 people to the store when his first album came out. Every time after that, the place has been filled to capacity. It's always fun to tell the crowd only eight to 12 people came that first time—and I see all of those people here today."
>
> —JOHN KUNZ, WATERLOO RECORDS, AUSTIN

jazz and blues festivals so patrons can enjoy a Sunday brunch with artists from the Delmark label. Bob Koester owns the label and the store, and finds that the brunch brings in different customers than he usually sees.

Criminal Records in Atlanta has an in-store stage larger than the ones many bands appear on at their proper gigs. J&R Records in lower Manhattan has gone so far as to close streets to present bands—Green Day attracted 6,000 people to a free show for the release of *21st Century Breakdown.* To support their 2009 release, they also performed at a Hot Topic store in Fargo, North Dakota.

Grimey's, a hub for local bands in Nashville, uses its stage to support them. It has hosted signings by the likes of Costello, Brian Wilson, and David Byrne. And as a thank-you for their support, Sharon Jones and the Dap-Kings gave a secret show in the store's basement.

"It's all about giving people a reason to come in," said Grimey's co-owner Doyle Davis. They keep the impetus high by hosting as many as 22 in-stores per month.

When the Downtown Music Gallery in New York moved to Chinatown from the Bowery, their concern was having a space large enough to continue presenting leading avant-garde musicians almost weekly. They settled on their new location partly because it afforded them that opportunity.

"One of the first things we did was make sure it was cool with our neighbors," said co-owner Bruce Lee Gallanter. "We're downstairs from a Buddhist temple and they chant a lot. We had to make sure it wouldn't disturb them."

The Amoeba stage in Hollywood is in the back of the 43,000 square foot store. The stage is good sized and even quintets do not look cramped when doing a show. Some performers have even commented on their vantage point—the rows upon rows of CDs and vinyl.

Elvis Costello, who performed there in 2009 for the release of *Secrets, Profane & Sugarcane*, noted, "I like the way you're arranged in straight lines, you're all in alphabetical order. I see a few new releases over there," he said, waving his arm to the right. "And over there," he said while pointing to his left, "a few outtakes."

When the Patti Smith Group played Amoeba, guitarist Lenny Kaye saw an even deeper connection.

"At Amoeba, I was not only playing to people, but I was playing to all these records I love—you felt like you were part of the universe of people who made records before you. I remember hearing the Velvet Underground's first album and thinking 'wouldn't it be wonderful to make that noise on the guitar' and here I was looking at that album, playing to it. Those are totems and touchstones of history. It felt nice to return the favor."

Ruckus in the Rock Section

Not every in-store, though, goes smoothly. Barenaked Ladies told fans who attended a show at Cactus Music in Houston that they were allowed to steal items that day. Electric Fetus in Minneapolis had to give away 300 copies of Redman's *Doc's Da Name 2000* when the rapper was a no-show.

ONE NIGHT ONLY: JOE STRUMMER

Joe Strummer arrived at Music Millennium without a band and managed to deliver an in-store that owner Terry Currier considers the store's finest hour.

"He had never done one," Currier said of the former Clash guitarist-singer-songwriter, who was touring with the Mescaleros in 2001 when he visited Portland, Oregon. "He was having a kind of crappy day and he comes onstage and asks 'anybody play the guitar?' A lot of hands go up and he asks one person to come up. 'Anyone drum? You come up here and be the drummer.' The first song was improvised. He sang the story of his day. It's the only time that song would have ever been played."

Strummer died Dec. 22, 2002 at the age of 50. But during 2001 and '02 when he did in-stores, he played those with the intensity he delivered at the proper gigs. "He played every show like it was his last," his publicist and friend Tresa Redburn said.

Warner Bros. Records got calls from Tower Records in New York the day after a Green Day in-store to see if they would be interested in picking up the tab for damages to the store.

In Los Angeles, Tower Records was the dominating force for in-store signings and performances, attracting the biggest stars across all genres and styles. Luciano Pavarotti, Dolly Parton, Sheryl Crow, Raconteurs, and other major acts have met fans at the famed Sunset Boulevard location.

A PLEASANT BREAK FROM A TOUR

Eric Levin has staged so many in-store perfor-mances he says: "I've got a lifetime of special moments but I remember a Meat Puppets show that was just perfect. In 1993, they were on one of those H.O.R.D.E. package tours and they were kind of bummed out about the experience.

They weren't playing to their fans. They came here, played for an hour and a half just kicking out the jams in our parking lot. Kids, dogs, Frisbees. A couple of police officers pull up and get out of the car. They listened for two songs, saw there was no drama and left."

Two miles south, and located across the street from a behemoth of a mall, sat The Wherehouse. A chain with more than 300 outlets, it was a large innocuous store in a strip mall. It wanted to steal some of Tower's thunder. Booking a major act to do an in-store signing was deemed the trick.

In 1990, the Cure and Depeche Mode had their biggest fan bases in Los Angeles, thanks largely to KROQ, the radio station that had been home to new wave for more than a decade. Depeche Mode was playing a local arena and agreed to do a three-hour signing at The Wherehouse, starting at 9 p.m. on a Monday. Fans started lining up early Sunday morning.

By the time the band arrived, the line was nearly 20 blocks long; the crowd was estimated at 15,000 people, and 20 police cars were deemed not enough so a helicopter and another set of officers were sent in.

"There was no riot, but they brought out the riot squad," Bob Bell, a buyer for The Wherehouse, remembered.

All the police activity caught the attention of the local news. The anchors and reporters, all of whom referred to the star attraction as "a group called Depeche Mode," reported the story more from the angle of traffic congestion than a cultural occurrence.

The attendance was unprecedented, something that Sire Records' executive Howie Klein feared when the band was booked. "The idea of doing an in-store with Depeche Mode was something that I thought would be impossible," Klein said.

Problems arose within 15 minutes of the start. Security forces could not get the doors to close and control the flow of fans into the store, Bell said. Klein and the members of Depeche Mode panicked. "We thought we heard windows being smashed in so we went out the back door," Klein recalled.

Bell was astonished by what he witnessed from the front of the store that night and in the aftermath. "I see the band being rushed out the back like a scene from *A Hard Day's Night*. There was minor property damage, but they had debates about this—Zev Yaraslovsky against Richard Blade. A county supervisor—a politician—against a local DJ. Come on."

Daniel Glass, whose career has included stints at major labels and the independents Artemis and Glassnote, was working for Chrysalis Records in the mid-1980s. Billy Idol had already scored a significant hit with his first album after leaving Generation X and was onto his second solo record, *Rebel Yell*, when Glass was guiding his career at the label.

Bill Aucoin was managing Idol at the time. Aucoin got into management after a stint in television and the first act he financed and developed was Kiss. His plan was to use Kiss-like elements to promote Idol.

"He didn't just want a crowd, he wanted pandemonium," Glass said of Idol's in-store signing at the lower Manhattan Tower store. "We got a radio station involved and it was insanity. The crowd broke the main window. I was scared. All hell was breaking loose and I didn't know what to do. Bill, he loved the craziness."

And sometimes the craziness is caused by the artist. Licorice Pizza booked the Plasmatics to do an in-store signing in Hollywood. The New York band was famous for their stage antics—blowing

Wendy O. Williams of the Plasmatics is pictured at Licorice Pizza in the early 1980s.

up TV sets, taking a chainsaw and cutting into whatever was available—and the attire of lead singer Wendy O. Williams was often removed during concerts. Most photos of Wendy show her topless with black electrical tape on her nipples.

"It's packed with people jumping on glass cases and I'm totally freaking out," recalls Lee Cohen, who worked in the Licorice Pizza front office at the time. He was the lone official on hand. "It was absolutely out of control. Wendy starts taunting the audience, then jumps on a case and rips off her clothes. A kid jumps on a case and drops his pants. I'm really surprised the cops didn't show up."

Most in-store performances, though, are peaceful, like the time the two Johns in They Might Be Giants serenaded customers as they wandered through the aisles of Record Service in Champaign, Illinois.

In August 2007, Currier had to close the Music Millennium outlet that housed more than 300 shows

THE ART OF THE IN-STORE

Stepping into Fingerprints in Long Beach, California, means taking a trip through one of the more impressive histories of in-store appearances of the recent past.

Besides the usual artifacts, knickknacks, and posters hyping albums, more than 50 silk-screened posters advertising events at the store line the walls: Neil Finn of Crowded House, Jonathan Richman, Patti Smith, John Doe, Joseph Arthur, Pete Yorn—a who's who of alternative and punk rock legends.

The posters began in 1997, the fifth year of Fingerprints' operation, and by the middle of 2009, art for nearly 200 in-stores had been printed. Each poster, many of them painted by established concert poster artist Robert Pokorny, is given to attendees who purchase CDs or vinyl, and then signed by the artists who are usually unaware beforehand that art has been created in their honor.

"They get here and we show it to them and since they're usually not expecting it, they're impressed," Fingerprints owner Rand Foster said. "But they're cool with it because it makes the in-store special."

Damien Rice has done only one in-store performance in his career. It was at Fingerprints. A live CD was made from the show.

Besides Rice, Fingerprints has released about a dozen CDs of in-store performances by the likes of the Hold Steady, Cold War Kids, and Rilo Kiley.

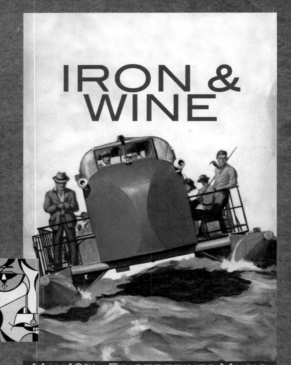

In-store performance posters for Fingerprints (right) and Gomez by Robert Pokorny.

when the landlord asked for a rent increase. The store was not showing a profit but Currier and his neighbors were keenly aware that the in-stores were attracting 25,0000 to 30,000 people annually to a shopping district they otherwise would not visit.

The record store transformed an unseemly neighborhood into a retail hotbed. Once the store closed, others went out of business, too. "Some blame the economy, others attribute it to us," Currier said. "The clientele that was going to that neighborhood was ours; the boutiques and restaurants got new customers from us."

Closings can have their cheery moments, too. Members of Crazy Horse, Hayes Carll, and Chuck Prophet delivered an impromptu show at Open Mind Music in San Francisco on its final day of operation. "I was riding by on my bike, saw that it was closing, and just put together some performances," Prophet said, who wrote about the day on his blog. "Hayes and his band finished their sound check up the street and just came in carrying their instruments."

That store closed on a high note, just like Village Music in Mill Valley. John Goddard put up the closed sign one final time on Sept. 30, 2007. He had first announced the final day in January, figuring it would take him nine months to reduce his inventory. Many of the performers who had visited to sing, sign autographs, or shop wanted to make a last appearance. Cooder and Costello performed as did DJ Shadow, the Bay Area turntablist. Rather

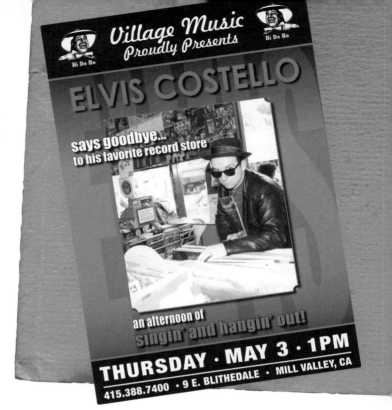

Elvis Costello was one of the last performers to appear at Village Music in Mill Valley, California, to honor the closing of the store in 2007.

than taking a specific time slot, DJ Shadow visited the store daily throughout the entire month of September and spun vinyl for up to three hours a day.

On its final day, the store was kept open for 24 hours. "We had thousands of people passing through. And (mandolinist/local resident) David Grisman walks in with his band, sets up in the corner, and plays. That last year was my most fun year," Goddard said. "I had a ball."

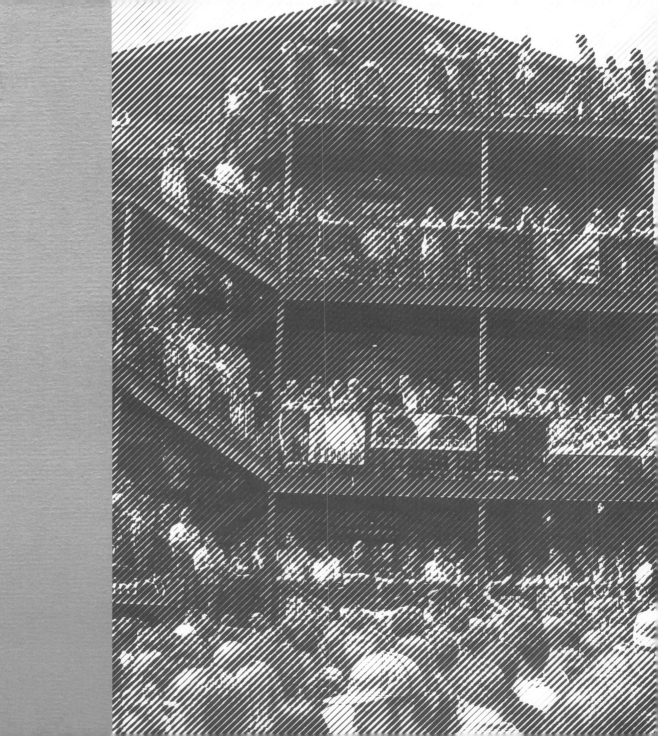

REDEMPTION SONG

IN 2008, RECORD stores created a "hook" to alert the media and the public that a closed sign was not hung in every store's window. Record Store Day was created, and the response was an enormous shot in the arm.

When it came time for a second Record Store Day—April 17, 2009—both retailers and labels greatly expanded their involvement. There was even an international element. By offering specially minted exclusive records, most of them singles, stores participating in the promotion were able to expand their business exponentially.

Independent record stores create a holiday in 2008 and stars add to the festivities

"The 'cool' record store. . . . is where you can talk to people who are like you. They look like you, think like you and, most tellingly, like the same music as you—the only comparable experience these days would probably be an art museum—an actual place where you can stand and simply be surrounded by your heroes."

—WAYNE COYNE OF THE FLAMING LIPS,
ON RECORD STORE DAY

Former Jayhawks leaders Mark Olson (left) and Gary Louris celebrated Record Store Day 2009 with Waterloo owner John Kunz (in Record Store Day T-shirt).

"The first year I was a lot more safe and I bought conservatively and records flew out of the store," said Paul Epstein, owner of Denver's Twist & Shout. In 2009, "I bought everything aggressively. Business was everything we could have hoped for."

In Nashville, Grimey's New & Pre-Loved Music staged a daylong concert that bounced between a variety of genres—rock, bluegrass, R&B, and, of course, country. The bill included the Avett Brothers, MuteMath, Del McCoury, Black Joe Lewis, and Charlie Louvin, attracting 3,000-plus people.

"Far and away it was our biggest day ever," co-owner Doyle Davis said, adding that business was 43 percent better than their previous best day. That record-setting day was the first national Record Store Day, held in April 2008.

The idea of a special day to celebrate record stores was created at a meeting of several coalitions that unify independent record stores. Chris Brown, the vice president of operations

In 2009, Grimey's attracted its biggest crowd and had its biggest sales day ever on the second Record Store Day.

at Bull Moose, which has 10 locations in Maine and New Hampshire, suggested the "holiday" and organized the event along with the Music Monitor Network, the Coalition of Independent Music Stores, Alliance of Independent Media Stores, and Newbury Comics.

By throwing parties and offering exclusive products that would attract fans and collectors, the organizations created an event that got a fair amount of media coverage the first year and an avalanche in the second.

"The first year of Record Store Day," said Terry Currier, owner of Music Millennium in Portland, Oregon, "newspaper editors were asking reporters to find out 'are there still record stores?' I read *The New York Times* and see that we're on the verge of extinction."

Scott Register of Junketboy Distribution/CIMS in Birmingham, Alabama, told the *Athens Herald-Banner* that Record Store Day "was our answer to the overriding opinion in the press that we're going away sometime soon."

Metallica kicked off the event's first year with an autograph session at Rasputin Music in San Francisco. Gov. John Baldacci gave a State of Maine proclamation in support of Record Store Day.

The biggest hurdle for Record Store Day president Michael Kurtz was getting a number of stores to believe in the promotion. "Nasty emails

The iconic sign of Rasputin Music in Berkeley, California

Metallica kicked off Record Store Day in 2008 at Rasputin in Berkeley.

poured in from store owners who were so bitter over what had happened over the last 10 years. They were tired of being disenfranchised. I think that 90 percent of the 50 or so people who wrote wound up apologizing."

With satisfied record store owners on board, Kurtz and his team targeted an international expansion in year three, formalizing the process so that collectible items can be manufactured and distributed overseas.

Stores Are Mobbed

For year two, Mayor Michael Bloomberg issued a proclamation making April 18 Record Store Day in New York City. Stores were stocked with 82 exclusive releases, and 600 live performances took place to commemorate the day.

Manhattan's Other Music was sold out of its stock of exclusives by 1 p.m. By midday, most of the stores involved had done as much business as they had the entire first Record Store Day.

There were lines everywhere: Vintage Vinyl in Fords, New Jersey, had 300 people waiting when it opened; 400 people went to Bull Moose in Portland, Maine, many of them waiting since midnight to meet members of the Disturbed.

Brandi Carlile, who records for Columbia Records, used her Record Store Day appearance at Graywhale in Salt Lake City to not only profess a

A ONE-OF-A-KIND COLLECTION

Twist & Shout in Denver, hailed by many as one of the top stores in the country, went with a product-heavy approach to the second National Record Store Day.

"I purposely took it easy on the events," said storeowner Paul Epstein.

He had something that no one else involved in the promotion could conjure up: a freshly purchased, and rather impressive, jazz collection. The approach was to unveil it on Record Store Day in the style of an auction house dealing in an art or fine wine collection.

Owner of the collection was Monk Montgomery, a jazz bassist out of Indianapolis who had performed and recorded with his brothers—guitarist Wes and vibraphonist Buddy—along with a host of other leading jazz musicians. He moved to Las Vegas and founded the Las Vegas Jazz Society in the early 1970s, which he was involved in until his death in 1982.

"I had been hearing rumors about this collection for years from his stepson, a local musician, and it took quite a while to convince him that we should sell it," Epstein said. "I had

never publicized a collection before, even ones I had bought from semi-famous people. So we kind of promoted it as Monk's and the response was great."

Of the 2,000 albums in the collection—nearly all of it jazz with a few blues and African titles mixed in—about 20 percent were mainstream. "The rest was completely weird. Some really out music. Private pressings, one-of-a-kind albums. A lot of it was signed 'To Monk.'"

Paul Epstein, owner of Twist & Shout in Denver, poses with a stand-up of Rick James.

A 2007 publicity still from the Breeders shows them shopping for records at Gem City in Dayton, Ohio.

fondness for vinyl, but she pledged to release her next album on LP two weeks before it is available as a download or a compact disc. She said the LP would only be sold at independent record stores.

Sky Saxon of the Seeds made it to Antone's Record Shop in 2009, just two months before he died.

The team that founded Record Store Day created criteria to keep out corporate entities and online e-tailers. Stores that made the cut, organizers said, have control over their stock, store policies, and promotions.

To participate, a store has to be a physical retailer that carries at least 50 percent music. The store's ownership has to be at least 70 percent located in the state of operation, and the company that owns the store cannot be publicly traded.

"In a weird time in this industry, this was a bright spot," Twist & Shout's Epstein said. "In spite of all the odds, [and] the difficulty this industry has had in generating excitement, it was a home run both years. It did not feel like a giant sellout."

Chris Cornell, Disturbed, Ra Ra Riot, and the Black Lips were among the bands that performed at record stores. Twin sisters Kim and Kelley Deal personally hand-screened the artwork for the Breeders' *Fate to Fatal* vinyl EP. The sisters made an in-store appearance at Shake It Records in Cincinnati.

Wilco members signed copies of their DVD *Ashes of American Flags* in Knoxville, Tennessee. In St. Louis, DJs manned turntables and bands performed at Vintage Vinyl; Euclid Records had a day of concerts beginning with the Bottle Rockets.

Stars Lend Support

Many leading artists lent their support by offering public comments about the importance of record stores. Paul McCartney, Bruce Springsteen, Peter Gabriel, Neko Case, and John Mellencamp were among those who chimed in, as did Tom Waits, Jack White, and Brett Gurewitz of Bad Religion.

Billy Bob Thornton, the drummer, singer, and songwriter in the Boxmasters—who happens to have also appeared in a fair number of films—

SEVEN INCHES OF FUN

Here's a look at some of the limited edition vinyl singles that were released on Record Store Day in 2009:

Bad Religion. *Bad Religion*, a new edition of their 1981 debut EP with a photocopied, handwritten lyric sheet.

Camera Obscura. "French Navy," which opens the album *My Maudlin Career*, backed with the non-album track "The World Is Full of Strangers."

Bruce Springsteen. "What Love Can Do" 7-inch, backed with "A Night with the Jersey Devil."

The Decemberists. "The Rake's Song" backed with the unreleased "East India Lanes."

Bob Dylan. "Dreamin' of You" backed with a live "Down Along the Cove."

Lykke Li/El Perro Del Mar. Split between Li's version of Wendy Rene's "After Laughter (Comes Tears)" on one side and El Perro's "(At Your Best) You Are Love" on the flip.

MC5. "Kick Out the Jams" backed with "Motor City Is Burning."

Tom Waits. A medley of "Lucinda" and Leadbelly's "Ain't Goin' Down to the Well" backed with "Bottom of the World," all recorded live during his "Glitter and Doom" tour.

Grizzly Bear. "While You Wait for the Others" backed with their version of the Phil Spector non-hit "He Hit Me (And It Felt Like a Kiss)," recorded at KCRW in Santa Monica.

spread his story on National Public Radio's *All Things Considered*. Thornton grew up in Malvern, Arkansas, and would visit Paula's Record Shop to flip through 45s and albums. "We couldn't afford to buy anything, so we would just hang there all day— it was really like Oz to us. I got my entire musical education from that record store and the radio.

"When I'm out on tour or on location, I'll find whatever independent record store is around, and that's where I'll go. Independent record stores are really the only places left with the actual spirit of music as I knew it growing up, and hopefully, they'll be around 50 years from now," Thornton continued. "Because that's where it feels magical:

You don't feel like you're buying a tire iron, tube of shampoo, a 12-pack, a bag of Cheetos, and a record."

Comments from musicians ran the gamut—memories of shopping, personal connections with store employees, philosophies behind supporting physical products, local ownership, and enthusiastic sales clerks who are living a dream being surrounded by music.

"The independent record store isn't just some place where geeky vinyl dudes get their rocks off. It is the focal point of your local music scene," George Pettit of Alexisonfire wrote. "It is the focal point of all local music scenes. It is where you find out about upcoming concerts. It is the birthplace of thousands of musical junkies. If the future of music is free of indie record stores, we might as well . . . give up on culture altogether."

A few artists singled out their favorite stores. Stanton Moore of Galactic touted his relationship with the owners of the Louisiana Music Factory in New Orleans; Jason Lytle of Granddaddy saluted Cactus Records in Montana; and Train's Pat Monahan gave a shout-out to Raspberries record store in Erie, Pennsylvania. Rocky Votolato expressed an affinity for his hometown stores of Sonic Boom Records and Easy Street in Seattle. Josh Clark of Tea Leaf Green shared his fondness for now-shuttered Southern California stores Moby Disc in L.A. and Middle Earth in Downey.

Jeremiah Edmond of Manchester Orchestra heaped praise on the shops he visited as a teenager while touring: 52.5 in Charleston, South Carolina, Criminal in Atlanta, and Manifest in Columbia, South Carolina.

On the international side, Jack White singled out Membrane in Germany; Luka Bloom was big on Concerto in Amsterdam; and Adam Duritz of the Counting Crows allots at least half a day on every trip to London to visit Minus Zero and Stand Out Records. White called on his peers to embrace the physical: "Show respect for the tangible music that you've dedicated your careers and lives to, and help it from becoming nothing more than disposable digital data."

Hayley Williams, the lead singer of Paramore, lamented that the Tennessee store she shopped in starting at the age of 12 was closing a month before Record Store Day. "It's a shame Franklin [Tennesse] will not have a record store," she said during an in-store performance at Cat's Music. "This says a lot about the community."

David Was and Don Was of Was (Not Was) issued a statement with a similar message. "In the beginning was the record store, more like a modern-day temple with its attendant priesthood and initiates, a holy repository of the culture's most sacred beats and rhymes. By comparison, the Internet is a clean room in a hospital—it lacks the

The Louisiana Music Factory in New Orleans is a favorite record store of Stanton Moore of Galactic.

funk and feeling of a place with floors and ceilings and racks full of soul-stirring goodness."

On the Flip Side

Coverage of Record Store Day, while certainly boosting the profile of independent music retailers, brought to light some of the gripes the independents have with the majors.

Paul Olszewski of Paul's CDs outside Pittsburgh, Pennsylvania, was among the many storeowners pointing out that vinyl—new and used—is the item keeping stores in business. As he told *The Pittsburgh Post-Gazette*, that does not mean he and the indie ilk get to corner the market.

When U2's *No Line on the Horizon* was released on vinyl, Olszewski saw it as a smart risk. "They were limited to 7,000. Best Buy got 5,000 of those;

2,000 copies were allotted for the rest of the country. My salesperson at the distributor was allotted five. We got one or two."

New York magazine felt the flaw in Record Store Day was that it targeted people old enough to be sentimental for vinyl and brick-and-mortar shops, and did not do enough to bring in the kids who have never purchased music according to the size it comes in: 7 inches or 12 inches.

More significant than providing goods that would promptly wind up on eBay with price tags 400 percent higher than the initial price, the faux holiday was instrumental in restoring the notion of a record store's importance in a community. For those who have worked behind the counter for years and decades, not to mention the musicians who have been on both sides, the day is a reminder that the record store is a hangout, a community

MEANWHILE, RELEASED ON CD . . .

Two of the hottest compact discs released for Record Store Day came from My Morning Jacket and Queen. My Morning Jacket's *Celebración De La Ciudad Natal* was a seven-song, 45-minute live album recorded in the band's hometown of Louisville, Kentucky, and *Queen's First EP* was a CD reissue of a 7-inch vinyl compilation initially released in 1977.

center, and a place to interact with like-minded people. It's a place where guidance and advice is free and not connected to computers.

Music Millennium's Terry Currier pointed out "our industry never reacted to downloading well

and once those habits developed, there was nothing they could do."

To power through the digital revolution, Currier has become one of those leading lights in a grassroots movement of music fans and purveyors who bond over the popular and obscure, people who thrive on the discourse. The modern version of the American record store is a combination of the entrepreneurial and curatorial in both skills and spirit.

"There's plenty of niche left, vinyl has decades left in it," noted Eric Levin of Atlanta's Criminal Records. "And if (labels) don't produce things for our customers, we'll do it. That's why we have buckled down and see bright skies ahead. That's why we created Record Store Day."

An all-vinyl store in 2010 is not that different from the Commodore store of the late 1930s. Whether they were curating indie jazz during World War II or the indie rock at the turn of this century, the stores that survive and the ones starting anew are driven by taste and knowledge.

Few stop to think about their role in this continuum. Yet every shopkeeper who opens their doors is demonstrating faith in music as a tangible item to be cherished, even handed down from generation to generation. That keeps music alive.

TOP RECORD STORES ACCORDING TO THESE PUBLICATIONS

Since the inception of Record Store Day in 2008, several publications have compiled lists of the country's finest record shops.

Spin. Amoeba, Hollywood, San Francisco, and Berkeley, California; Waterloo, Austin, Texas; Other Music, New York, New York; Wax 'N Facts, Atlanta, Georgia; Sonic Boom, Seattle, Washington; Ear X-Tacy, Louisville, Kentucky; Aquarius, San Francisco, California; Grimey's, Nashville, Tennessee; Music Millennium, Portland, Oregon; Wuxtry, Athens, Georgia; Reckless, Chicago, Illinois; Goner, Memphis, Tennessee; Electric Fetus. Minneapolis, Minnesota; True Vine, Baltimore, Maryland; Record Exchange, Boise, Idaho

Paste. Amoeba Music, Los Angeles, California; Criminal Records, Atlanta, Georgia; Other Music, New York, New York; Cat Head Delta Blues & Folk Art, Clarksdale, Mississippi; Waterloo Records, Austin, Texas; Aquarius Records, San Francisco, California; Dusty Groove America, Chicago, Illinois; Ernest Tubb Record Shop, Nashville, Tennessee; Shangri-La Records, Memphis, Tennessee; Music Millennium, Portland, Oregon; Ear X-Tacy, Louisville, Kentucky; Louisiana Music Factory, New Orleans, Louisiana; Newbury Comics, Boston, Massachussetts; Grimey's New + Pre-Loved Music, Nashville, Tennessee; Turntable Lab, New York, New York; Electric Fetus, Minneapolis, Minnesota; Jerry's Records, Pittsburgh, Pennsylvania

GQ. Princeton Record Exchange, Princeton, New Jersey; Vintage Vinyl, Fords, New Jersey; DJ Hut, Washington, D.C.; Philadelphia Record Exchange, Philadelphia, Pennsylvania; Magnolia Thunderpussy Records, Columbus, Ohio; Aquarius, San Francisco, California; Waterloo, Austin, Texas; Amoeba, Los Angeles, California; Ear X-Tacy, Louisville, Kentucky; Other Music, New York, New York; Good Records, New York, New York; Turntable Lab, Los Angeles, California; AKA Music, Philadelphia, Pennsylvania; Voltage, Asheville, North Carolina; Reckless Records, Chicago, Illinois; The Thing, Greenpoint, New York; B-Side, Madison, Wisconsin; Honest Jon's, London, England; Rare Records, Sacramento, California; Domino Sound Record Shack, New Orleans, Louisiana

Rolling Stone. Amoeba Music, Los Angeles, California; Dusty Groove, Chicago, Illinois; Waterloo, Austin, Texas; Other Music, New York, New York; Vintage Vinyl, Fords, New Jersey

Vinyl, In-stores Popularize a New Holiday

Less than a week had passed after the fourth celebration of Record Store Day on April 16, 2011 when the reviews started pouring in. "Best day in 12 years," said one retailer. "Best day in 25 years," another countered. "Last year's Record Store Day was beat by noon," was a common, cheerful response.

One hundred people were in line when Mark Bunnell opened his store, the Record Exchange, in Boise, Idaho. Head of the Coalition of Independent Music Stores, a Record Store Day organizing group, he attributed success in year four to in-store events—Foo Fighters at Fingerprints in Long Beach, California; a reunion of the dB's at Criminal in Atlanta, Georgia; Regina Spektor at Other Music in New York City—and the national press that started reporting when Ozzy Osbourne was named RSD ambassador.

Vinyl was the dominant format on Record Store Day Four, with no package larger than the Flaming Lips' "Heavy Nuggs: The First Five Warner Bros. Records 1992-2002." Flaming Lips leader Wayne Coyne explained the day's appeal: "No one knew all the dimensions of experience you were having when you used to buy records. You got to hold it, you put it on a record player, watched the needle hit the vinyl. You didn't know you were participating in something that was a shared experience and, little by little, we have seen all the

The Foo Fighters rock Fingerprints in Long Beach, California, for Record Store Day 2011.

dimensions of that experience disappear. Flaming Lips can have a say in extending that experience because Record Store Day is around. [It's] for people who truly love music the most, which lets us make something special."

In 2010, highlights included the Bull Moose chain in Maine and New Hampshire hosting performances in all ten of its stores with acts such as Grace Potter and Circa Survive. Smashing Pumpkins played a gig in Hollywood, California, for Amoeba; the four bands that played in-store performances at Radio-Active Records in Fort Lauderdale, Florida, had exclusive releases for the day; and Minus the Bear premiered new songs at Sonic Boom in Seattle, Washington.

Record Store Day Releases

The third annual Record Store Day took place April 17, 2010. Among the special releases were live CDs from Band of Skulls, Grace Potter & the Nocturnals, Manchester Orchestra, Paolo Nutini, One Eskimo, and Tegan & Sara. Omnivore Recordings, the first record label to launch on a Record Store Day, offered Big Star's "Third" LP on vinyl and a Buck Owens 45.

Split 45s, in which two acts are represented on one single, were popular; pairings included Bon Iver/Peter Gabriel, Jakob Dylan/the Courtyard Hounds, and the Budos Band/Sharon Jones & the Dapkings.

A John Lennon set of three singles was among the special packages. Others included a four-LP Wilco box set "Kicking Television"; a Joy Division "Box Set" of four LPs; a Coheed and Cambria picture disc; numbered Elvis Costello and the Attractions "Live at Hollywood High" EPs; R.E.M.'s "Chronic Town" on blue vinyl; and two Sonic Youth reissues—"Confusion is Sex" on white vinyl and "EVOL" on pink vinyl. Built to Spill, Devo, Fanfarlo, Hole, Muse, the Rolling Stones, and Bruce Springsteen released 45 RPM singles.

Among the LPs released were: The Apples in Stereo, "Travellers in Space and Time"; Beach House, "Zebra"; Jeff Beck, "Emotion & Commotion"; Deerhoof's, "Apple O'" and "Green Cosmos"; Hold Steady, "Heaven is Whenever"; Josh Ritter, "So Ruins The World Away"; Roky Erickson & Okkervil River, "True Love Cast Out All Evil"; and Tom Waits, "Mule Variations."

The fourth edition of Record Store Day featured a healthy collection of 45 RPM singles, many of them reissues. Among the acts represented were: 13th Floor Elevators, AC/DC, Ryan Adams and the Cardinals, Bad Brains, the Beach Boys, Blitzen Trapper, the Civil Wars, Death Cab for Cutie, Fela Kuti, Pearl Jam, Phish, the Rolling Stones, Rush, Bruce Springsteen and the E Street Band, and the Velvet Underground.

Specialty releases included 10-inch LP versions of Kings of Leon's "Holly Roller Novocaine" and Mumford & Sons/Laura Marling's "Dharohar Project," and a Beady Eye box set of seven-inch singles.

Vinyl LPs released for Record Store Day 4 included: "Bob Dylan in Concert: Brandeis University 1963"; Foo Fighters, "Medium Rare"; Ray Lamontagne, "Live Fall 2010"; Of Montreal, "The Past is a Grotesque Animal"; Regina Spektor, "Four From Far"; Television, "Live at the Old Waldorf" (2 LPs); Various artists, "Follow Me Down: Vanguard's Lost Psychedelic Era (1966-1970)." Among the reissues were the Grateful Dead's debut album in mono; John Fahey's "Requia"; Pink Floyd's "London 66/67" and Nirvana's "Hoarmoaning."

PHOTO CREDITS

We appreciate the contributions of the following people, stores, organizations, and companies.

Page 102, Courtesy of Jim Greenwood (Licorice Pizza billboard); Courtesy of Cary Mansfield (Mansfield at Wallichs)

Page 103, Photo by Adam W. Wolf

Page 106, © Henry Diltz (CSN, James Taylor); © Henry Diltz, Courtesy of The Morrison Hotel Gallery (The Doors)

Page 108, Courtesy of Music Millennium

Page 110, Courtesy of Schoolkids Records

Page 111, Photo by John Huffman, www.huffmanimage.com

Page 112, Courtesy of David Henderson/ www.AzioMedia.com

Page 113, Photo by Jason Kramer

Page 114, Photo by Sam Epstein

Page 115, Photo by Jason Kramer (Rhino 45); Photo by John Huffman, www.huffmanimage.com (Aron's Records)

Page 116, Photo by Gary Calamar

Page 117, Courtesy of Hulton Archive/Warner Bros/ Getty Images

Pages 118–119, 121, Courtesy of Peter Jesperson

Page 123, Photo by John Huffman, www.huffmanimage.com (Recycled Records); Courtesy of Amoeba Music (Robyn Hitchcock)

Page 124, Photos by John Huffman, www.huffmanimage.com

Page 125, Photo by Sam Epstein

Page 126, Photo by Jack Pierson

Page 127, Photos by John Huffman, www.huffmanimage.com

Page 128, Courtesy of Gary Calamar

Page 131, Courtesy of Amoeba Music

Page 133, Photo by Henry Rollins (Yesterday and Today); Photo by Sam Epstein (Nels Cline)

Page 134, Courtesy of Hale Milgrim

Page 135, Photo by Gary Calamar

Page 137, Courtesy of Hale Milgrim

Page 138, Courtesy of Music Millennium (Currier cassettes); Photo by Jason Kramer (Twin/Tone CD)

Pages 140–141, Courtesy of Antone's Record Shop

Pages 150–151, 152, Photo by Gary Calamar

Page 153, Courtesy of Hale Milgrim

Page 155, Courtesy of Criminal Records (Levin and store); Photo by Gary Calamar (Foster)

Page 156, Courtesy of Antone's Record Shop

Page 160, Courtesy of Waterloo Records

Page 162, Courtesy of Other Music (Other Music); Photo by Alice Calamar (Dusty Groove)

Page 164, Photo by Tim Soter

Page 165, Courtesy of Downtown Music Gallery

Pages 168–169, Courtesy of George's Song Shop

Page 170, Courtesy of Amoeba Music, Artwork by Wayne Shellabarger

Page 171, Courtesy of Amoeba Music

Page 172, Photo by Gary Calamar

Page 173, Courtesy of Music Millennium, Photo by Issa Sharp

Page 176, Photos by Gary Calamar

Page 179, Courtesy of The Music Coop, Photo by Scott Calamar

Pages 182–183, Courtesy of George's Song Shop

Pages 184–185, Photo by John Huffman, www.huffmanimage.com

Page 187, Photo by Josh Anderson

Page 191, Photo by John Huffman, www.huffmanimage.com

Page 193, Photo by Jason Kramer

Pages 196–197, Photo by Josh Anderson

Page 198, Courtesy of Amoeba Music

Page 200, Photos by Sam Epstein

Page 201, Courtesy of Waterloo Records

Page 203, Courtesy of Music Millennium

Page 205, Photo by Josh Anderson (Phoenix); Courtesy of The Michael Ochs Archives/Getty Images (Patti Smith); Photo by Adam W. Wolf (James Brown)

Pages 206, 207, Courtesy of Music Millennium

Page 211, Photo by Adam W. Wolf

Page 212, Posters by Robert Pokorny, Courtesy of Fingerprints Records

Page 213, Courtesy of Village Music Archives

Pages 214–215, Photo by Lisa Ray

Page 216, Courtesy of Waterloo Records

Page 217, Photo by Lisa Ray

Page 218, Photo by Steve Jennings/Wireimage/Getty (Metallica); Photo by Pete Cutter/Alamy (Rasputin)

Page 219, Courtesy of Twist & Shout Records

Page 220, Photo by Chris Glass

Page 221, Courtesy of Gary Calamar

Page 223, Photo by John Huffman, www.huffmanimage.com

Page 224, Courtesy of Record Store Day

Page 226, Photo by JED

INDEX

Note: Page numbers in *italics* refer to photographs.